My Life's Journey
a memoir

My Life's Journey
a memoir

Ted T. Tsukiyama

WATERMARK
PUBLISHING

© 2017 Ted T. Tsukiyama

All rights reserved. No part of this book may be reproduced in any form or by any electronic or mechanical means, including information retrieval systems, without prior written permission from the publisher, except for brief passages quoted in reviews.

ISBN 978-1-935690-89-4

Library of Congress Control Number: 2017936224

Author royalties on sales of this book support Nisei veterans organizations.

Photography courtesy Ted T. Tsukiyama except photos on pp. 82, 121 and 122 from the Hawaii War Records Division/University of Hawai'i Archives and Manuscript Collection.

Design and production
Ingrid Lynch

Watermark Publishing
1000 Bishop St., Ste. 806
Honolulu, HI 96813
Toll-free 1-866-900-BOOK
sales@bookshawaii.net
www.bookshawaii.net

Printed in the United States

Contents

Part One • The Early Years — 1

Tatsuya, Tedde-San and Ted
Our Genealogy
My Family
Growing Up in Ka'imukī
School Days
Japanese Language School
Roosevelt Rough Rider
The University of Hawai'i

Part Two • The War Years — 30

December 7
The University ROTC
The Hawai'i Territorial Guard
Varsity Victory Volunteers
The 442nd Regimental Combat Team
The 522nd Field Artillery Battalion
Military Intelligence Service
Shipping Out
Postscript to War

Part Three • The Postwar Years — 94

Back to School
Indiana University
Yale Law School
Marriage and Family

Part Four • A Lawyer's Life — 112

Family Man
My Private Practice
Alternative Dispute Resolution
The Art of Bonsai
Community Historian

Appendix — 155

Writings and References
Feature Articles

Preface

By God's benevolent grace, I have survived nine decades going on ten, in good mind and health. I have tried to give back as much of the bounty as I have received, and in that spirit I feel I should share my version of a generation's story. It is the story of Americans of Japanese ancestry who were born after World War I, were raised in the Great Depression, served and fought in World War II and who thereafter contributed to the national prosperity and success into the twenty-first century.

Nationally, we were a despised minority who were of the same ancestry as the enemy. Yet in even the worst moments in Hawaiʻi, prejudice and discrimination were tempered by an inclination to accept people as people and to make friends across racial and ethnic barriers. From such beginnings, we conclusively demonstrated our loyalty as Americans and went on to be among the country's most successful minority groups. I believe that in this process, we contributed to the democratization of America.

Part One

THE EARLY YEARS

Tatsuya, Tedde-San and Ted

The Hawai'i State Department of Health's vital statistics show that I was born on December 13, 1920, of parents Seinosuke and Yoshiko Tsukiyama, with the given name of "Tatsuya." My mother's life story mentions that I was named "Tatsuya Ted" but the name "Ted" does not appear on the birth certificate. I do not recall being called by my Japanese name except at Japanese language school. Also, I remember being called "Tedde-san" by villagers when I visited Japan as a little boy of six. Otherwise I was always called Ted and legally have been known as Ted T. Tsukiyama.

My mother gave birth to me at the family residence at 1042 17th Avenue in Ka'imukī with the aid of a midwife. I assume the birth was normal, since I have not suffered any congenital birth defects or diseases. I lived and grew up in that 17th Avenue house. My three older siblings were likewise born at home: brother James Keiichi, born May 25, 1915; sister Naoko, born November 28, 1917; and sister Kazu, born January 13, 1919. Only our younger sister, Martha Masako—on October 6, 1923, was born in a hospital.

Our parents' memoirs tell us that our births were registered at the Japanese Consulate in Honolulu. Our names were probably also entered in the *koseki tohon* (family register) in Japan. This registration made us citizens of Japan, resulting in citizenship in both the United States and Japan.

As tensions of a possible conflict between Japan and the United States increased in the late 1930s, our parents renounced our Japanese citizenship with the Japanese Consulate. This was possibly one of the positive factors considered by the FBI in not classifying Dad as a "dangerous enemy alien" to be hauled away to a concentration camp after Japan's attack on Pearl Harbor.

Our Genealogy

Our family roots can be traced back to samurai who served under Toyotomi Hideyoshi on the Tsukiyama side and under the Heike army of the Taira clan on the Kagawa side.

On the Tsukiyama side, we can trace back nine generations to our ancestor Tsukiyama Keiemon, who died February 26, 1730. According to my father Seinosuke's memoirs, his grandmother said that Keiemon was a retainer of Lord Hirano, a warrior who served under Hideyoshi and was known for his bravery in battle. The next seven generations were: Tsukiyama Edaemon; Tsukiyama Denzaemon; Tsukiyama Naoyoshi (Edaemon); Tsukiyama Naoteru (Edaemon); Tsukiyama Naoyoshi (Edaemon); then coming to Tsukiyama Naohiro (Edaemon) who married Rui, my great-grandmother, who had four children: Ito, Fumi, Naotada and Chiyo (my grandmother, 1853–1907).

Seinosuke's memoir says his grandfather was a samurai who defended the shores of Uraga when Admiral Matthew Perry landed in Japan. He was awarded a certificate recognizing his bravery. His offspring Chiyo married Kawakita Masajiro, a wholesale charcoal dealer who lived in Hacchobori, Kyobashi-ku, Tokyo. They had nine children, of whom my father Seinosuke (January 1, 1890–November 4, 1978) was the seventh.

Despite the fact that Seinosuke was born a Kawakita, Chiyo made him take the Tsukiyama family name because there was apparently no male to carry the name forward. This changing of names to perpetuate family lines was a fairly common practice of the times.

The Early Years

My father and his siblings all went to a private elementary school and were taught good manners, discipline and Chinese classics from a strict principal. Seinosuke recalled that his grandmother Rui enjoyed listening to recitals of his piano lessons. She could tell if he skipped anything, and she didn't allow him to go out to play until he finished his studies.

Of my father's siblings, I may have met Uncle Shotaro when I visited Japan as a boy. I am sure that I met Uncle Shinichi Kawakita, who worked for a Japan company in New York in the 1930s and who often stopped off in Hawai'i on his travels. Uncle Shinichi had a son, Koichi, my cousin, who is now living in Tokyo and is the only close family relative on the Tsukiyama side still living in Japan today with whom I have contact.

Interestingly, the family genealogy chart shows that my parents were related to each other by marriage (but not biologically) through the following family ties: my grandmother Chiyo's older sister gave birth to a daughter (Dad's cousin), who married a Kagawa, who was the eventual uncle of my mother. In short, my parents Seinosuke and Yoshiko were already related to each other even before they got married.

On my mother's side, the Kagawa ancestral lines can be traced back only a few generations. But according to her memoirs, her roots went back into the fifteenth century to a Kagawa Kagenobu, a leader of the Taira clan (Heike) army, after whom the Kagawa Prefecture (Kagawa-ken) in Shikoku was named. After the Taira were defeated by the Genji in 1581 at Dannoura, Kagawa Kagenbu escaped and secreted himself from the Genji on the Inland Sea island of Shiwaku Hiroshima in the village of Enoura. He disguised himself, working as a farmer under the assumed name of "Hirao" and thereafter created a long line of Kagawas, most recently traceable two generations ago to one Kagawa Tokishi, who is my mother's grandfather, thus my great-grandfather. Kagawa Tokishi died at the early age of thirty-six but left behind four children, three boys and a girl. The second son was Kinshiro, my maternal grandfather. Kinshiro Kagawa was a Shinto temple carpenter, which may account for my skill with the hammer and saw! Kinshiro Kagawa (1859–1930) married Taki Oka (1870–1948) and they had one child, my mother Yoshiko. She was born in 1895 and lived to be ninety-two years of age.

My Family

My father's memoirs omit mention of his childhood up to the time he left for Hawai'i. Before I did my research, I did not know he was one of nine children nor do I recall him ever talking about his parents or his siblings, except for the Uncle Shinichi who we got to know. I knew only of the wholesale charcoal business in Tokyo (which makes him a true "Eddokko" or native of old Tokyo) and also that he was smart enough—and his family had means enough—for him to attend the elite Keio University, from which he graduated in 1908. Somewhere along the line he attended *yagaku* (night school) to learn English. Because the school was run by Christian missionaries, it was inevitable that the fishhook of Christianity was imbedded in his English lessons. He was soon converted and became a member of the Ginza Christian Church. He taught Sunday school and was one of the few Christians among the Japanese who immigrated to Hawai'i in the early 1900s. Father came to Hawai'i at the suggestion of his cousin Michi Kurasawa Isoshima, who invited him to work in the Isoshima stores. He sailed on the *Tenyo Maru* and landed in Hawai'i on August 11, 1911.

My father's reluctance to say much about himself contrasts to his considerable detail about my mother Yoshiko's early background. She was born on February 5, 1895, the only child of Kinshiro and Taki Kagawa, on the island of Hiroshima, Kagawa-ken. Her parents already were living in Hawai'i but her mother (my grandma Taki) just happened to be in Japan at the time of giving birth to her. As a result Yoshiko was technically an Issei (first-generation immigrant to Hawai'i) but effectively was Nisei (second generation). She returned to Hawai'i with Grandma Taki on November 25, 1899, at age four. They lived at the Isoshima Shoten on King Street, near the corner of Bethel Street in downtown Honolulu. She recalled being threatened by flying sparks from the Great Chinatown Fire of 1900, which fortunately stopped one block away from her. She attended Castle Kindergarten, Normal School and Royal Elementary School. She attended Sunday school at the Japanese Christian Church on River Street. In 1905, her father moved to Wahiawa to raise pineapple next to the Dole family, and she remembered playing with the Dole children.

In 1906, at age eleven, Mother was sent back to Japan, where for three years she attended Shuntai Eiwa Jyogakko, a Baptist missionary school. She then transferred to Ferris Jogakuin Seminary in Yokohama and graduated in 1913. Ferris was a Christian-sponsored school, so most likely she became a Christian while at Ferris. Seinosuke's parents were her guardians while she attended school in Japan, which is probably when Seinosuke first met his wife-to-be. In her memoirs she writes: "Seinosuke was five years older than I and did not pay any attention to me." She returned to Hawai'i in March 1913 on the *Tenyo Maru*, at which point Seinosuke had been here for two years. By then her father had quit pineapple farming in Wahiawa and had moved to Kapahulu Avenue, where he started a poultry farm. She worked as a salesgirl and seamstress at the Isoshima Hat Store on King Street while Seinosuke was employed at the Japanese Bazaar by his sponsor, Kunosuke Isoshima.

According to one family elder, it was Seinosuke's cousin Michi Isoshima who suggested that Yoshiko would be a good match for Seinosuke. Seinosuke's version in his memoirs says, "The Isoshima and Kagawa family thought it would be suitable for the future of the Isoshima Shoten business for Yoshiko and me to be married. They talked to me about this idea and it took some time for me to answer after considering it from all angles. There was no love affair involved, so I had time to observe the situation with very cool insight…first, she was very healthy and had a very pleasant disposition. With both English and Japanese educational background I felt she would be my ideal person as a wife. We had been acquainted for a long time and known each other's background well enough. So I decided to marry her and, to keep the Kagawa name going, agreed that the first son born to us would bear the Kagawa name."

My mother wrote that she had several marriage prospects that her father turned down. Her family agreed on my father, provided that the firstborn male child would keep the Kagawa name. "We were really not in love in a romantic way," she wrote, "but had no objection to this marriage." Both being Christians, they were married at the First Japanese Methodist Episcopal Church on River Street in Honolulu by Reverend Chuzo Nakamura on August 17, 1914.

They lived in the rear cottage of the Isoshima residence on 10th Avenue in Ka'imukī for a year. Meanwhile, Grandpa Kagawa retired and in 1915 purchased the three lots on 17th Avenue for fourteen cents a square foot. He built a residence on the third lot, where both he, Grandmother and my parents lived. This was to be the family home for the next forty-five years. Grandpa Kagawa worked at the Japanese Bazaar as a handyman until he and Grandma Kagawa decided to retire to their home in the village of Enoura, Kagawa-ken, in 1920, just before I was born.

My father served as manager of the Japanese Bazaar for the Isoshimas for thirty years, until he opened his own gift shop, the Hale Makana, in 1941, just before World War II started. Our family life centered around the Japanese Bazaar, which was located on Fort Street near the Pauahi Street intersection.

The employees were like one big family, so we Tsukiyama kids participated in many company parties, picnics and social events. Dad went to work daily, while Mother was always the good housewife. She kept us well fed, well clothed and healthy, as Dad credited and complimented her for in his memoirs.

He described his child-raising philosophy in his memoirs as follows: "The children grew up under Christian influence and according to their natures. I believed that the children were sent to us by God, so we as parents were not supposed to have our way but love and respect each one of them the way God had intended. So that when they grew up they would be worthwhile in contributing something for the community. I can say we raised them rather leniently, never scolded or spanked them much and gave them freedom. So in a way it could be said that there was not strict discipline and in those days it could have been viewed as spoiling them, but we thought it was the best way to help bring out their good points."

What children could be so lucky as to have a parent with a mindset and attitude like that, but we Tsukiyama kids did!

Where so many of my peers' fathers were domineering disciplinarians, I was fortunate that my father was an even-tempered, kind person. He was a gentleman in the truest sense. I can't ever remember seeing him angry, losing his composure or resorting to force. Just imagine, I don't recall ever getting a spanking from him!

I would not be overstating when I say no one could ask for any finer and greater parents than I had, and I wouldn't trade them for anyone else in the world! I could not have become the person I am without them. Our family has grown up into a loving, close-knit family only because of our parents' loving nurture. Their hard-earned means was devoted to us five children, never to themselves. They saw to it that all of us got a college education. In turn, it must have been gratifying to them that none of us gave them problems.

Christian faith was the rock upon which my father built his life. He confessed in his memoirs that he became bored and without ambition for the future in his work at Isoshimas, but then he was suddenly struck by the Bible verse that says, "Seek you first the Kingdom of God or you will not enter heaven; even though you possess the whole world if you are not a righteous person what good will it be." He wrote, "Now I began to realize that though one may get rich by making money and rise to success, it will not please God. Not material things but understanding and following God's will is more important. You will be blessed and you will be loved by both God and man and be able to bring happiness to others. After these deep thoughts came to mind, I became a different person, now lighthearted and able to carry on my daily work happily. I was never so happy as at this time of revelation…"

Father's memoir goes on: "In looking back over my past fifty years in Hawaii, I have been a member of the Christian church and did my best to practice Christianity in my daily life. Materially I have nothing special to boast about, but have been blessed with bountiful daily food, enough to wear, with good health, a good wife, besides five children and eleven grandchildren. What a blessing!"

My father lived and practiced his Christian life quietly. Once I was interviewing Raku Morimoto, one of the saints of Harris Methodist Church and also Seinosuke's dear friend. The interview was about church history. She told about the hard times our church had gone through, particularly during the Great Depression of 1929, when many members lost their jobs. We were in danger of losing the church. So the treasurer of the church went to the bank and mortgaged his home to pay the minister and church expenses, thereby rescuing the church from bankruptcy.

"That treasurer was your father," Mrs. Morimoto said, "Seinosuke Tsukiyama!" I was astounded, but so proud! Who would be so foolish as to risk his own home to save his church? In fact, that is exactly what old Kunnosuke Isoshima told Seinosuke: *"Baka! Sonna baka na koto suru mon ga aruka*! (You damned fool! Who would do such a damned fool thing as you did!)" That treasurer was a *baka* all right. He was a baka for Christ! It is the highest honor to be the son of a man like that. As Mrs. Morimoto shared her story, we both shed tears. Hers were tears of nostalgia at the memory of those hard days and what her good friend Seinosuke had done for his church seventy-eight years previously. Mine were tears of pride.

I can never be half the man he was, nor can I ever hope to be a fraction of the Christian he was, but I am proud to be his son! There are still many people in town who think I am the son of that famous Hawai'i senator and Supreme Court chief justice, Wilfred Tsukiyama, but my unequivocal answer to that is, I wouldn't trade my father Seinosuke for any senator or chief justice in the world! It seemed to me my father was universally respected. He had no enemies. My parents died with very little in material things because they invested it all in their five children!

We Tsukiyama kids were likewise lucky to have a one-of-a-kind mother. As I indicated, she was only technically an Issei but really a

Nisei, living all but a few years of her life in Hawai'i. Because she was well educated, she helped with our homework. She read, wrote and spoke fluent English, and English was spoken at home. She also contributed to our meager learning of Japanese. From childhood, she was a baptized Christian. She was a devoted, loyal and supportive wife to Father for their sixty-five years of happy marriage together.

They were the consummate married couple, setting a model for the children to follow. I can't recall hearing harsh or angry words ever pass between them in their long life together. In his memoir, Seinosuke pays quiet tribute to Yoshiko, citing, "What your mother has gone through to bring you up in good health. It was not easy to bring five children into the world in ten years' time." When we were afflicted by childhood epidemics or little scrapes, "she was a nurse and doctor we could depend on. Fortunately with her knowledge of both Japanese and English (unlike many other women from Japan), we subscribed to English magazines and through the *Ladies' Home Journal* articles, she learned much on how to care for babies and bring them up properly."

Father continues: "She was very careful about how to dress the children. Besides washing, cooking and all other chores, she sat down to sew the girls' dresses and enjoyed it. She was pleased to see them dressed well. In those days the clothes were all homemade, not like the ready-made apparel you can now buy in shops. Every stitch was done by mother's hands and I admire her for the love and work she put into the things she made."

I remember only two instances where our parents experienced distress over us. Both had to do with Japan. One was after Grandpa Kinshiro died in 1929 at Enoura, when Dad and my sister Naoko went to Japan to bring Grandma Taki back to Hawai'i. But Grandma wasn't ready to leave the village, so it was decided that Naoko would stay back with her. Naoko was only ten or eleven years old at the time, and she was lonely and cried every night. This was probably the most miserable year of her life.

The second instance involved my brother Jimmy in 1939. Jimmy was a pioneer Nisei in the field of aeronautical engineering, but no American aviation company would hire a Japanese, not even Hawaiian Airlines. So in 1940 it was suggested that he go to Japan to look around. He got stuck after Japan's surprise Pearl Harbor attack and spent the entire war and a few years thereafter in the enemy country. Our parents never heard from Jim or anything about what was happening to him for the war's duration. They silently and stoically endured, but this must have caused them a great deal of anguish.

Now a brief summary of my siblings. As I said, by prior agreement Jimmy's last name was Kagawa, to perpetuate the Kagawa family name. From childhood, Jimmy was a model airplane hobbyist and an amateur radio operator. As a result of his technical and mechanical aptitude he was admitted to the Guggenheim School of Aeronautics at New York University in the mid-1930s. After getting stuck in Japan during the war, he was drafted into the Japanese Army pursuant to his dual citizenship. One good thing befell him. His unit was sent to Taiwan, which was then part of Japan's empire. There he met the family of Nihei Okazaki, Grandpa Kagawa's friend from the Wahiawa pineapple farming days. Okazaki had a lovely daughter named Hajime, who became Jimmy's wife. There was no question of their surviving the war, because American forces never attacked Taiwan.

He was ever reluctant to relive or to share his wartime experience. It took several years for him to repatriate to Hawai'i and regain his American citizenship. Once back in the fold of the United States, he went to Los Angeles, where broad opportunities in the aeronautical field were available with companies like North American Aviation and Hughes Aircraft. His wife Hajime worked for Japan Airlines as a ground hostess. They lived in Gardena, then Torrance, where they raised Patricia Keiko and Alan. Around 1998, they pulled up stakes and moved to Corvallis, Oregon, to be near Alan. They built a nice home in a wooded area outside of Corvallis and lived out a peaceful, well-earned retirement.

The number two sibling, my sister Naoko, was only two years older than I, and we always got along well. When we kids took turns cleaning up after the evening meal, she was my dishwashing partner. The many photos in the family albums show Naoko active in every phase of family life, with the exception of her unhappy year in Japan. She was well liked by her peers. She was a pretty and popular girl at the university and had many would-be suitors among the BMOCs (big men of the campus), such as one Masayuki Matsunaga, later better known as US Senator Sparky Matsunaga, who used to try date her. She studied at the Teachers College, and for her first teaching job she was assigned to a two-teacher elementary school in the forlorn "sticks" of Kalapana on the Big Island. She brushed off her various suitors and settled on a quiet country boy from Kauaʻi named Yoshiharu Ogata. As I was writing about her, Naoko called to say that "Ogie" just died after a long, slow deterioration of health. He was a good and faithful husband and provider to Naoko; a fine father to their children, Jon and Joy; and a caring grandfather to their three grandchildren and one great-grandson.

Sister Kazu, born in 1919, was my immediate older sibling, and as such she must have hassled me and vice versa during our childhood. Our mother liked to tell a story of when I was six years old visiting Japan. I went around telling everybody, *"Hawaii dewa Kazu to yuu wari yatsu ga iru.* (Back in Hawaiʻi there is a bad one named Kazu.)" Kazu was more boyish and athletic than Naoko and was known as a good tennis player up through her high school years. Like Naoko, she was popular in school. Up to the time she married, she studied to become a social worker. Although there were many available Japanese boys around, Kazu married Ralph Vossbrink, who at the time was a union activist in local labor circles. I attended their simple wedding at Waikīkī during wartime. Interracial marriages by Japanese women were still rare, but our parents to their everlasting credit made no fuss about it and graciously accepted Ralph into the family. We watched with pleasure and pride over the years as she and Ralph raised their four good-looking *hapa* children: Tony, Mark, Muffi and Lisa.

After me came our little sister Martha, who was quieter and less assertive than her older sisters. I was scolded often because I teased Martha and made her cry, as when I imitated the squeaky sounds that emanated from her violin. During the war years, we four older siblings were out of the house, and Martha was the only one at home to care for and comfort our worried parents. At war's end, she attended MacMurray College in Illinois and worked on the Mainland for a while before coming home. We remember well that after Grandpa Tsukiyama died in 1978, Martha devoted herself at the cost of a free life to caring for Grandma for the next nine years until Grandma died. The rest of us will always remember this classic demonstration of *oya koko* (filial devotion) to Grandma to the very end by our "kid sister." We are eternally grateful. Martha had never married up to then but after Grandma's death Joe Giovanelli re-entered her life. They married, and thereafter she lived a peaceful and happy life with Joe in Maryland near Washington, D.C.

Growing Up in Kaʻimukī

Dad took a lot of photos of the family, leaving me with a visual trail of my childhood years. The earliest photo of me was taken as an eight-month infant in Mom's arms. Until Martha came along, there are a number of photos of me with Mom, which shows that she was pretty close to me during that time.

At twenty-five months I wandered off and stuck my right foot in a dying fire of mango leaves, and one of Dad's photos shows me recuperating in my wooden horse rocker with a bandaged right foot. Somehow I can still visualize the glowing embers beneath the top layer of gray ashes and also remember my screams of pain. There are a number of shots of me with brother Jimmy and my sisters, most notably one of us sitting on the running board of a Ford Sedan taken about 1925 in what must be our first family car. I am shown in many group photos taken at family gatherings and the company picnics, usually at Kailua Beach. There is only one photo to remind me of my Japan trip in 1926, showing me and a bowlegged pup in front of Japanese pines.

Up to grammar school age, I had a terrible temper that could be triggered at the slightest provocation. I got the nickname *obake*, which means monster or demon. Jimmy and his friends loved to tease me to trigger the obake image, and I used to chase after them, throwing stones and cursing them at the top of my lungs. Today people who take my Buddha-like calm and patience for granted simply cannot believe that I was once a terrible little brat.

Father took several photos of me with the neighborhood kids, like Donald "German Doughnuts" Napier, Bobby Metcalf and Clifford Anderson. We lived in a racially mixed middle-class neighborhood, with the Napiers and a part-Hawaiian family as immediate neighbors. The Metcalfs, Camaras and June Lee's family lived across the street, and the Asahinas and Matsuis at the corner of Pahoa and 17th Avenue. On Harding Avenue were the elder Fernandez couple with orphaned Charlie Warrington (Hawaiian) and also the Hegenbergers, McQuerys and Fraziers. On 16th Avenue there were the Brunners immediately behind us and Helen Eveleth's family, later the Marlowes and Doris Maloney's family, and next the Kunanes, Silvas and Andersons, all of whose kids used to play with us. If anything, it was a predominantly *haole* neighborhood, but we got along fine, without a trace of racial friction or discrimination.

The one exception was a kid named Elliott, who lived on Pahoa Avenue. He was considered snooty, and we hated him with a vengeance. Our gang, which consisted at the time of myself, German Doughnuts, Bobby and Charlie, built a clubhouse in the mango tree in our front yard. Underneath we dug a hole lined with *kiawe* thorns and covered it over with branches. The idea was to lure Elliott to step into the trap when he came around. We also pissed in a quart milk bottle, which we kept up on the tree. We saved it until it ripened into a fermented brown elixir, ready to pour on poor Elliott. Glenn Fukuda was a younger boy from a nearby business family from Japan. Glenn used to hang around us, but when his mother heard about the proposed urinary shower, she banned her son from playing with "those bad boys on 17th Avenue!"

Usually we engaged in more wholesome activities, such as cowboy and Indians, baseball and football. We played Olympic sports such as high jump, pole vault and broad jump in pits we dug in the empty lot across the street. German Doughnuts, Charlie and Bobby were all bigger than I, but I was older so I used to boss them around as *kodomo taisho* (juvenile general).

My childhood trip to Japan with Mom and Martha lifted me out of the neighborhood for nearly a year. This was 1926, when I was five. Mom was seasick most of the trip over and stayed in the cabin with Martha while I roamed the ship by myself. I faintly recall arriving in Yokohama and visiting Dad's home on the banks of the Sumida River in Hacchobori, Tokyo. We must have been hosted by Dad's brother Shotaro. Then we went down to Shikoku to the village of Enoura on the small island of Hiroshima in the Inland Sea, where we stayed with Grandpa and Grandma Kagawa for almost a year. I remember going to school in the rear part of the village and playing with the village kids, who called me "*Hawaii no Tedde-san.*" According to Mom, I was one of Grandpa's favorite people. Every day he clipped grapes off the vine and we ate grapes together. I bossed those other kids around, and I predicted great things for myself in the future ("*Kono yatsu wa taishita mon ni naru zo*"). I don't recall being homesick or missing Hawai'i at all.

By the time we returned home, I had forgotten all my English. Jimmy used to be embarrassed when he took me on the streetcar and I jabbered to him in a loud voice in Japanese. In Mom's memoir she writes that I could not immediately take the entrance test for Aliiolani School, an English Standard school. By September, I had recovered enough to pass the test and enter the first grade. Strangely, my ten months in Japan did not enable me to distinguish myself in a scholarly way at Japanese school.

About a year later, when Yoshie Isoshima got married to Takeo Isoshima, I was shanghaied into the wedding party as the reluctant ring bearer. The wedding photo shows the lovely bride along with Mom as matron of honor, Martha as one of the flower girls and the only male, me, with a dour face holding the ring cushion in my lap. It made me appear as if I were wearing a skirt. I felt like a big sissy. But Yoshie-san was always one of my favorite people, so I guess I begrudgingly endured the sacrifice for her sake.

The Early Years

This was about the time of the infamous Fukunaga case, which shook the entire community. A mentally deranged Nisei, Miles Fukunaga, kidnapped the Jamieson family's son for ransom and killed him. This brought great shame upon the Japanese in Hawai'i. It was as if being Japanese made us complicit in the crime. It also caused extreme tension and anxiety as the police searched for the murderer among the Japanese youth in the community. I distinctly remember my parents telling me to come straight home from school and not to loiter in public, where enraged crowds were psyched up into a lynching mood.

There followed the Great Depression years starting in 1929, when the entire community suffered through a failed economy. The Depression financially ruined many people in Hawai'i, but I cannot recall that our family endured any deprivation or hardships. Dad kept his job with Isoshima Shoten, enabling him to provide for his family. We attended school, studied and lived a normal life.

As I moved into middle school years, I joined the YMCA Friendly Indians club and attended YMCA summer camp at Camp Erdman. I was a Boy Scout with Troop 9, in which I worked my way past the Star badge. Later I surfed at Waikīkī, making my own ten-foot redwood surfboard and also a hollow, laminated surfboard that leaked. In my high school years, I was a pitcher for the Roosevelt junior baseball team coached by Jim Lovell, who during the war years was to serve as executive officer of the famous 100th Battalion. I also played second base for the B.K. Yamamoto baseball team in the American Legion Baseball League, where I met several guys—Sus Yamamoto, Chiyoki Ikeda and Barney Ono—who I later served with during the war.

As I grew into high school I was no longer tethered to the Ka'imukī neighborhood, and my friends changed accordingly. I had no close Japanese friends. Instead my gang consisted of haole like Earl Smith, Alfred Smythe, Eugene Girdler, Harry Holt and Art Stubenberg. I used to get invited to their homes and even slept over and had meals with their families. One of them had a car so we used to go joyriding around the island or to Mokapu Beach (where the Kāne'ohe Marine

Base now is) for bodysurfing. This is where one of them took a photo of me bare-balls as I was changing into my clothes.

One time we tried to crash a high school party at the Waimānalo Shriners and got into serious trouble. We got shut out, so we pissed in the gas tanks of their cars in retribution. We sped away, chased by our angry victims up toward the Makapuʻu Lookout and then down toward Sandy Beach. Our car couldn't hold the curve and we rolled, shooting over the road bank into the kiawe bushes. I got a bump behind my right ear, which luckily was our only injury!

In high school we didn't go out with girls. I had my first date ever when I had to take a partner to attend our graduation dance at Waialae Golf Club in June 1939. I was really socially immature and naïve as far as girls were concerned in those days, but I tried to make up for lost time when I got to the university!

One of the usual questions asked in oral history interviews is whether religion played a part in the growing-up experience of the interviewee. My own early church life is attested to by a photo in which Dad is holding me as a year-old infant, with the congregation lined up on the steps and porch of the old wooden Japanese Methodist Episcopal Church on River Street, overlooking Nuʻuanu Stream. I remember nothing about that church structure, because we moved when I was four to Fort Street and Vineyard Boulevard and became known as Harris Memorial Church. For several years, I detoured into the Sunday school at the Epiphany Church on 10th Avenue close to our Kaʻimukī neighborhood. I used to walk there with my friend German Doughnuts Napier.

During my high school years, I was back at Harris Church for Bible classes under John Young, who as a youth worker at the Nuʻuanu YMCA was well known in the community. To Young, I must attribute my basically pragmatic, mundane perspective on Christian theology. We weren't expected to believe in the miracles of Jesus where, for example, "walking on water" was possibly a matter of walking on a sandbar, or where the miracle of the loaves and fishes could have happened because it was the custom for everyone to bring his own bread and fish bento when they went out into the field. To this day I cannot accept, or should I say tolerate, the charismatic approach to biblical interpretation or to church ritual and service.

I simplistically see the value of the Bible in the call to follow, adapt and apply Christ's teachings to our daily lives; to pursue moral, ethical and spiritual enrichment; and to become better human beings. I support my church with tithes and service, but I am not a fraction of the great Christian that my father was, and I never will be.

Recently someone interviewing me remarked with surprise how different my story was compared to most Nisei. In terms of our relationship with the surrounding society, the fact that our parents were both converted and baptized Christians from Japan was a rare departure from the norm. I always thought that being in a Western religion definitely must have eased the acculturation and Americanization process for us children.

Our blessings and advantages were multiplied by our parents' educational backgrounds, my mother as a Ferris Jogakuin Seminary graduate and my father as a graduate of Keio University, with both being able to read, write and speak English. Education, combined with their grasp of English, was a boon that hastened our flow into the cultural mainstream of America.

It also mattered that I did not have the negative experience of plantation life that so many of my Nisei peers dealt with. In the main, the Hawai'i of my early years was still highly stratified into social and racial hierarchies, with the haole always lodged at the top. Nisei who grew up in plantation camps or villages or in urban Japanese ghettos like Palama or Mō'ili'ili had little or no contact with haole. This nurtured feelings of inferiority towards haole and a consciousness of "knowing your place." In contrast, my experience growing up in a racially mixed middle-class neighborhood like Ka'imukī, which included a lot of haole, allowed me and my family to live without any feelings of inferiority to, or social awe of, haole. I always assumed that I was just as good as (and in some cases even better than) my haole peers.

Even more fortunately, I cannot recall ever experiencing any case of racial slight, condescension or prejudice by any of the haole people in my daily contacts. While I did not come from a "silver spoon" background, my good fortune of growing up in such a healthy social environment must have unconsciously and unknowingly affected and influenced the social outlook and attitudes with which I faced my later life. For this I am most thankful.

I greatly value the sense of tolerance these positive influences endowed in us. For example, the Japanese community was notorious for esoteric condescension against people from other prefectures, particularly Okinawans, but in our family we grew up not knowing what or who an Okinawan was, much less that they were to be looked down upon or ostracized.

To give another example, one of my father's best business friends was a "Mr. Goldman," who was fond of us and treated us warmly. Only after I went to the Mainland did I realize that Mr. Goldman was a caricature of the Jewish merchant of Venice. I also had two African Americans in my class, Marie Buffins and Patty Smith. Patty was the most popular girl in school and even now tells people she had a crush on me at school!

School Days

Our parents strongly believed that we should receive a good education, and all five of us got a college education, probably at a considerable financial sacrifice on their part. For this we owe them a lot. We in turn have insisted that our children and grandchildren be afforded maximum educational opportunity. I cannot recall our parents ever having to nag or insist that we do our homework and do well in school. We did so with the conscious knowledge that without education we would never achieve anything or amount to anything in life. Sadly, this is not the case with today's generations.

Even before going to Japan in 1926, I recall being sent to Castle Kindergarten on King Street, where the City Municipal Building now stands. It was the premiere preschool institution of its time. During my year's stay in Japan, I remember going to the first grade in Enoura village. On my return to Hawai'i at age six, I was fortunate, as I've indicated, to get into an English Standard school (Aliiolani Elementary School) despite my recent immersion in Japanese.

In the view of its many critics, the English Standard system was a not so subtle discriminatory effort by the then dominant haole elite to provide public schooling for their kids, free of any contaminating influence by local kids who spoke only pidgin.

Pidgin was not an obstacle for me because heavy pidgin was not spoken in Ka'imukī, although somewhere along the line I learned to speak it with the best of them, as it is a second language essential to getting along in Hawai'i. True to the pictures painted of English Standard school, my few class photos from Aliiolani show the student body was predominantly haole. For example, in Mrs. Peterson's 1929 third grade class photo, I can identify only three Asian faces and names: Carol Wong, Sachiko Noda and me. In addition, I recognize Dorothy Lorenz, Anna Cleveland, Pearl Knott, Lokelani Davenport, Eleanor Walker, Pearl Nunes, Jane Kirby, Mildred Wood, John Toomey, Douglas Caldwell, Harold Skinner, Mervin Gilliland, Jens Schultz, Johnny Morrison and Bob Dye; in all, eighteen haole, three part Hawaiians and two Portuguese.

Nonetheless, I was never conscious of being Japanese. I remember being cast in a Thanksgiving Day enactment of "The Courtship of Miles Standish," in which I was cast as none other than Captain Standish, commander of the Plymouth Colony. I put my heart and soul into my role with a mindset that my ancestors came over as pilgrims on the *Mayflower*.

My teachers were all haole. There was Mrs. Ferreira in the second grade, Mrs. Peterson in the third grade, Mrs. Johnson in the fourth grade, Mrs. Hurd in the fifth grade and Mrs. Marsland in the sixth grade. They treated all of us equally and taught us well, and I feel they gave me a good elementary school education.

While the main feature of my elementary school experience was rapid Americanization and a feeling of equality with all others, it was also about fun things that kids do. My first grade classroom was in a separate cottage down by the corner of Waialae and 6th Avenue, and during recess Bobby Morrison (part Hawaiian) and I would climb to the top branches of a Royal Palm tree, rocking and swaying the tree while we sang at the top of our lungs:

My fadda' is one bucha,
My mudda' cut da meat,
And I'm the leetle hot dog,
Dat run across da street!

In fourth grade while on kitchen duty, I was cleaning out the kitchen's cabbage-dicing machine when my KP partner Kenneth Weir (Portuguese Hawaiian) suddenly cranked the wheel, dicing my right thumb into a bloody mess. They bandaged me up at the dispensary and sent me home, and I had to walk all of the fourteen blocks to 17th Avenue. I arrived home weak and pale, to the utter shock of my mother.

The only time I ever played hooky was when a friend and I stayed all day at his home because we didn't want to wear pajamas to a costume day at school. For this I caught holy hell. In the first two years I served as a proud junior police officer (which was an honor in those days), making sure that the younger kids safely crossed Waialae Avenue. I don't recall distinguishing myself in scholarship while at Aliiolani but neither did I risk any possibility of flunking.

Japanese Language School

When I was six, I also started attending Ka'imukī Japanese School on 10th Avenue in Palolo. After finishing public school at two o'clock, I would walk about ten blocks home for a snack and pick up my Japanese books, then walk another twelve blocks to Japanese school in Palolo in time for the three o'clock bell, then walk home after school. I spent an hour each day with my Japanese lessons under a fiery Mrs. Akagi in the first grade and Mrs. Inokuchi in the second grade. In those days, almost every Japanese family sent their kids to Japanese school to learn the language and culture of Japan, but most of us didn't have our heart in it.

We mainly attended Japanese school to comply with our parents' wishes. I secretly resented the fact that I had to study Japanese when the non-Japanese kids were free to play the whole afternoon. We had double the homework at night, which further left us little time for recreation. Japanese school was designed to be highly competitive, rating and ranking us on our scholastic standing. I was only an average student. I never tried to compete for *yuutosei* (top scholar). The only time I can recall physical punishment from a teacher was when I was either late or absent because I had skinned my knee before school. I was slapped in the face by Uyehara Sensei, who later apologized when he noticed me limping around on my bandaged knee.

Besides lessons there was the *gakugeikai* (school drama), where we got to perform in front of our beaming parents. I forget the name, but one was a play about an old villager who spent years digging a tunnel to connect his village to the next village. The old man only got the off and on support of his fickle fellow villagers, who lacked his *nesshin* and *shinbo* (dedication and perseverance). I think Japanese language school was also where we learned and played out the story of the *Bakudan San Yuushi* (three bomber youth), in which three young Japanese soldiers volunteered during the Manchurian war to carry a torpedo into the enemy barbed wire barricade, blowing it and themselves up so that their fellow troops could rush through the opened gap to attack the enemy. All Nisei learned this heroic tale of devotion to country, which probably accounts in part for why there are several recorded *banzai* charges against the German enemy during World War II, all of them by the 100th Battalion and 442nd Regiment.

Pageants and *shibai* drama and the *shuushin* (morals and ethics) classes at Japanese school were a vital source of exposure to traditional Japanese values (*kachikan*). I think such teachings contributed to the basic character of the Nisei generation during those prewar years and distinguish us from the *sansei*, *yonsei* and *gosei* generations that followed.

For the six-year period from 1933 through 1939, I was sent to Hongwanji Chugakko, reputedly the top Japanese high school in Hawai'i. Male students were required to wear black coats and ties even in the hottest months. I faithfully attended four years of middle school and two years of senior high school. When class at Roosevelt ended at 2:30, I used to walk all by myself along an old dirt road, climb up a trail along the Papakōlea hillside behind Punchbowl to Round Top Road, and then walk down to Fort Street to the Hongwanji Buddhist temple. In the last few years my classmate Roy Ohtani had an old Chevrolet sedan, so I got a ride every day.

The curriculum consisted of reading and vocabulary, *sakubun* (creative writing), translation, shuushin (morals, ethics and traditional Japanese values) and later *kanbun* (Chinese characters), *soosho* (cursive writing), *soroban* (abacus) and the like. I rose no higher than the middle of *ichi no kumi* (class one) and often got dropped down to *ni no kumi* and *san no kumi* (classes two and three).

In those classes at Japanese school, I made most of my lasting Japanese school friends, who like me were just going through the motions. Those rascals did not treat me as a competitive rival but were good-fun companions. They used to irreverently give nicknames to our various *sensei*. The cross-eyed one would be called "Coggy," and the one who scratched his crotch would be referred to as "Scratchy." Not more than ten percent of the students seriously studied and competed for rankings while the rest of us showed up to "pay the *gessha*" (tuition) and to comply with parental wishes. Despite the fact that I attended twelve years of Japanese school (albeit only one hour per day), I would say that my proficiency level was second or third grade by Japan's education standards. For example, I never attained the competence to read all the *kanji* of a Japanese newspaper.

It was at Hongwanji School that I made one of my closest friends, Richard Sakakida, who was to become a legend. We sat next to each other for most of the six years. Sakakida turned out to be one of the greatest Nisei heroes of World War II. He was the only Nisei who was captured as a POW of the Japanese Army in the Philippines, enduring unspeakably cruel torture by his captors and yet never cracking to reveal he was an intelligence agent of the US Army.

Richard went to the heavily Japanese McKinley High School, and he was one of the McKinley students who used to regard those few of us Nisei who attended Roosevelt School as "high hat." Our Roosevelt ROTC uniforms had a green stripe down the side of the pants that made us stick out like a sore thumb at Japanese school and an object of derision. A lot of it became good-natured as we got to know one another, but I was nonetheless known as "Roosie" (from Roosevelt) at Japanese school. Forty years after the war was over, I finally located and wrote to Richard Sakakida. When he picked up my letter, the first thing he told his wife Cherry was: "Oh, this is from Roosie."

Roosevelt Rough Rider

I was automatically admitted to the English Standard Roosevelt School as a result of graduating from the English Standard Aliiolani Elementary. At the time, Roosevelt was both a middle school (seventh to ninth grade) and a high school. I started attending Roosevelt at its present Makiki location in 1933. My father dropped me off every morning on his way to work. Being English Standard, Roosevelt was predominantly (say seventy-five to eighty percent) haole, and was facetiously referred to by its critics as "a poor man's Punahou." My schoolwork was unremarkable, but neither did I encounter any real scholastic difficulties. Much of my junior high years are a blurred memory, partly—as I said—because Japanese school left no time for extracurricular activities and school social life.

Going over my Roosevelt High School senior class roster, I recall the racial makeup was roughly like this: fourteen Japanese plus one hapa (a beautiful girl named June Miller), five Koreans, fifteen Hawaiian/part Hawaiian, twenty-nine Portuguese, thirty-two Chinese and one black (Patty Smith), leaving about one hundred and eighty-eight haole, or nearly a two-thirds majority. You can see that the fifteen Japanese made up only five percent of the senior class. So it was definitely a haole school, and we in the minority must have considered ourselves privileged to be admitted.

I had tough but good teachers, notably Virginia McBride and Esther Friezell for English, Dorothy Gill for French, Fay McCartney for social studies, Margaret Frowe and Sarah Mathews for history and Helen Carter for mathematics. My seventh grade music appreciation class was taught by a pretty platinum blonde named Mrs. Irene Culver. I learned to appreciate classical music from that time on as evidenced by the A she awarded me. My teacher for Mechanical Drawing was a coach, James Lovell, who eventually became widely known in the community for going off to war with the Nisei.

In my 1939 yearbook, the *Round Up*, under my senior class photo is a single entry, "National Honor Society." I am one of about twenty-five seniors so recognized. Otherwise, you can't find me pictured in any of the school activities. I attribute this relative absence not to my temperament but to the demands of attending both Japanese school and public school.

I would have liked to try out for Roosevelt's athletic teams, but I was a frustrated would-be team athlete for lack of time. My version of athletics was confined to the ocean and to pick-up sports in the neighborhood. I was a swimmer from a moment in early childhood when my brother Jimmy pushed me into the Natatorium, the ocean swimming pool in Waikīkī. Furious, I churned to the surface and climbed out, so I could get back at Jimmy. As I grew up, I went through a period of several years hanging out in Waikīkī and surfing.

Despite my relative inactivity, my haole classmates accepted me as one of them, judging not only by my friends but also by the fact that I was chosen by my teachers and classmates as one of the four valedictorians to speak at our graduation ceremony in June of 1939. My valedictory experience deserves special mention, given that a thinly disguised purpose of the English Standard system was to minimize the contamination of haole by the local pidgin-speaking rabble and also minimizing students "of color" excelling scholastically. Some of my toughest teachers stood up against these practices, much to their everlasting credit. Serving as a graduation speaker was a great honor for me, if shocking, because I had not participated in extracurricular activities. Further, I was not one of the brightest of students. In historic context, my teachers made their choice against the backdrop of the war in Asia, which was a time of rising anti-Japanese distrust and prejudice. I have no other way of explaining how this happened.

I vowed to give the speech my best. I wrote it out, then gave it over and over until I could recite every word by heart. I remember going to Ala Moana Beach to practice, facing the ocean like the great Roman orator Cicero. It was titled "Hawaii's Youth Look to the Future," a copy of which I still have. It reflected the lofty idealism of the times, ending with the ringing phrase from "Ulysses" by Tennyson, "To strive, to seek, to find, but not to yield!" Come graduation night, I was nervous as hell, but I think it went well. I got lots of good comments. My public speaking debut was a success.

Notwithstanding that I came from a middle-class merchant's family, I went to work during summer vacations to pay for my books, supplies and clothes. Starting in 1937, at sixteen, I got a job at the Dole Pineapple warehouse through my mother's cousin Sam Oka, who was a big-shot *luna* there. I first helped the gang that stacked cases of canned pineapple and juice, and then I became a checker and counted the cases. Both of these jobs were better than actual labor inside the cannery. Our entry pay was thirty-five cents per hour, and by the time I quit after the 1941 season it was forty-two and one half cents per hour.

Summer cannery work not only earned me school expense money but also a bonus sex education. We worked with Filipino bachelors who on paydays would change into their dress clothes, fancy long sleeve shirts, pleated zoot pants that came up under their chest and tapered down at the ankle, shiny boots with two-inch heels and hair slicked back with heavy pomade, reeking with cheap men's fragrance. They would head off to their favorite whorehouse downtown. They would come back on Monday and regale us with their sexual exploits and conquests, with graphic instructions on the use of the "Spanish fly," feathered ticklers and the various positions to achieve maximum gratification. One guy named Slim used to brag that he would read a newspaper while he was getting his customary blowjob, and every Monday when he saw me, the innocent schoolboy, he would teasingly invite me with "You like go read da newspeppa' wit me?"

The University of Hawai'i

I started the University of Hawai'i (UH) freshman class in the fall term of 1939 as one of six hundred forty-seven freshmen, up to then the largest first-year class ever. Our introduction to college life was memorable in part because of the hazing inflicted upon us by the arrogant sophomores. They did mean things to the incoming frosh, like tossing various members of our class in the swimming pool, kidnapping us and locking us up in cages at the Waikīkī zoo, and taking us out to the cane fields of Waipahu and Waimānalo, with the goal of stripping us of our clothes and leaving us to find our way back to the city. I was considered one of the "leaders" of the freshman class especially targeted for hazing, and I remember hiding out at Kenneth Chang's home (he was McKinley class president) while the sophs came looking for me. Frosh Week was climaxed with the flag rush, where eager freshmen tried to climb the greased telephone pole to capture the sophomore flag, only to be pulled down and "de-pantsed" as they ran naked, seeking the safe refuge of the locker room past the crowd of delighted shrieking coeds.

The university student body of prewar years was predominantly non-haole, so at UH I made an entirely different set of friends. I found that you make your lifelong friends in college, not high school, and it was at UH that I made friends with the likes of people I have stayed in touch with, such as Kats Tomita, Claude Takekawa, Harry Tanaka, Herb Isonaga, Ralph Toyota, Buda Hamaguchi, Toshiyuki Nakasone and lots of *pakes* such as Kenneth Chang, Arthur Wong, Jackie Wong, Phyllis Tam, Rachael Leong and one Filipino, Adelino Valentin. Notice, not one haole.

According to the 1940 *Ka Palapala* yearbook (when I was a freshman and my sisters Naoko and Kazu were graduating seniors), I was elected as treasurer of the freshman class (Class of '43) and a member of the Freshman Class Council. By this time I was able to engage in more extracurricular activities because I was no longer burdened with having to attend Japanese school.

I remember History 100 and Political Science 150. They were huge classes, divided into two sections, and held in Farrington Hall auditorium. The history professor was Klaus Menhert, a German national. He made history meaningful, but the political science professor Paul Bachman was very dull.

Based on the entrance exam results and perhaps coming from an English Standard school, my written and oral English was good enough to skip English 101. I was put in English 102. It was focused on creative writing, taught by a Professor Neil, a martinet in the proper use of English. If I ever thought I was a good writer, I was quickly dissuaded by Professor Neil. It says something about my mother's devotion to English that she saved not only my finished papers but also drafts, so I have a large collection of Neil's cutting comments. For my painstaking explanation of "How To Make A Surfboard" he deflated me with: "Not really intelligible to me in great part." I was utterly devastated by his final critique of my "Memoirs Of A Sportsman" theme, in which he concluded: "Write shorter—cut out exaggerated diction, solecisms, and at least if you are to remain in 102 at all do not venture another glaring disagreement between number of subject and verb." He had a particular thing about subject/verb agreement, at another time writing, "Unpardonable error!" At yet another point he wrote, "You call this writing?"

I wrote an essay titled "Kokokahi," which was scarred with red ink but nonetheless bore a final comment, "Very Inspiring." To my surprise, he gave me an A-minus for English 102.

In retrospect, Professor Neil was the first to lay bare my deficiencies as a writer. I grant I take great liberties with the English language. I use or create words that cannot be found in Webster's Dictionary, and I tend to express and include too many thoughts and subjects into interminably long sentences. I still take unpardonable liberties with the English language in all my writings even to this day.

In addition to English 102, my other freshman courses were ROTC, Physical Education, Survey 100 and Oriental Studies 202. According to my UH report cards I got four As and three Bs for a 3.6 grade point in the first semester, but I fell to a 3.4 grade point in the second semester (too much extracurricular fun!).

In my sophomore year my report card shows that I took English 150, Anthropology 150, Economics 150, Psychology 150, Philosophy 150, ROTC and Physical Education for a total of eighteen credits. I wound up with a 3.0 grade point for the first semester and 3.5 for the second semester. There were no memorable or outstanding professors that I can recall. They were strict lecturers with no teacher-student dialogue whatever. The professor would come into the classroom, open his notes, lecture for fifty minutes, close his notes and be gone until the next class. They showed no personal interest in the student, and we were not invited to their offices unless it was for a chewing out. As a result, we became regurgitating automatons, placing a premium on note-taking, memorization and parroting the material for the exams. We were not called upon nor trained to examine, think or question. Asian kids excelled at this type of pedagogy, but this would not serve us well in later graduate schools where we were exposed to Socratic dialogue with the teacher or had to think on our feet. Such demands created traumatic situations for the UH-educated student!

With a limited amount of outside extracurricular activity, I maintained a B to B-plus scholastic standing while serving on the Sophomore Class Council, the Associated Student Council and the university YMCA club.

It was through the YMCA that I became acquainted with Hung Wai Ching. Hung Wai was executive secretary of the Atherton YMCA, and I became one of his "boys." He was probably responsible for appointing me as one of the Hawai'i delegates to the Asilomar Conference, a national gathering held each year on the scenic Monterrey Peninsula of California. The Asilomar trip was the highlight of my sophomore year at UH. It gave me my first chance to travel to the Mainland. As a Christian fellowship experience, the conference allowed me to meet sincerely warm and friendly Mainland haole people who regarded and treated us Asians as equals. Some continued to be my friends thereafter. After the conference ended, the Hawai'i delegation (Eleanor Matsumoto, Doris Ching, Kwai Sing Chang, Elbert Yee and I) went down to the Los Angeles area to visit YMCA groups at USC, UCLA, Redlands, Pomona, etc., which exposed us to *kotonks* (Mainland Japanese Americans) for the first time. This may have helped me to lessen the sociocultural shock that afflicted so many *buddhaheads* as they encountered kotonks for the first time at Camp Shelby at the outset of wartime training in 1943.

My junior year at UH began in September 1941. I loaded up with eighteen credit hours again, including History 201, History 242, English 250, Business 150, Political Science and ROTC. I completed my studies with four As and two Bs for a 3.66 grade point, my best scholastic effort at UH. The third-year ROTC was an advanced class through which I planned to earn a reserve officer's commission after completing 1942 summer camp training. In the meantime, I was appointed as first sergeant of the ROTC's Company B, captained by Nolle Smith.

On the extracurricular side, the 1942 *Ka Palapala* student annual reminds me that I was elected junior class president that year, which I had completely forgotten. The rest of the junior class cabinet was Kenneth Ching, vice president; Phyllis Tam, secretary (Phyllis was to finish the junior year as president in my place); and Vernon Jackie Wong, treasurer. My only other activity was UH YMCA treasurer, which must have further ingratiated me with Hung Wai Ching. The social highlight of the year must have been the junior prom but, for the life of me, I can't remember who my date was. Fatefully, the prom was held on December 6, 1941, a moment in which we were totally and blissfully unaware that Admiral Isoroku Yamamoto's attack fleet was stealthily steaming toward us several hundred miles north of Pearl Harbor, bent on a mission of total annihilation of the US military installations in Hawai'i. 🖝

Part Two

THE WAR YEARS

December 7

No one who witnessed the attack by Japan commencing at 7:55 a.m. on December 7, 1941, will ever forget that memorable day for their lifetime. December 7 will go down not only as the Day of Infamy but as the watershed date of the twentieth century. The attack drastically and irreversibly changed the course of my life and the lives of everyone who was of Japanese ancestry. It changed the history of Hawaiʻi, our nation and indeed the whole world.

I was trying to sleep off the rigors of the junior prom, but I was awakened by the sound of constant rumbling. Going outside, I saw the sky toward Pearl Harbor black with smoke, punctuated above by puffs of white aerial bursts. Like many people, my reaction was, "They're sure making this maneuver look real," but I turned on radio KGU to check it out. I heard the frantic voice of the broadcaster Webley Edwards screaming, "Get off the streets, take cover! We are being attacked by Japanese warplanes! This is no maneuver…this is the real McCoy! Take cover!" I felt like I was hit with a piece of shrapnel.

I experienced a series of changing feelings and emotions. First was a feeling of numb, shocking, uncomprehending disbelief. It was like a bad, bad dream: "This just can't be happening!" This soon turned to indignant outrage: "You damn fools, what do you think you're doing! You're just crazy to attack a great country like ours…

you'll never get away with it!"

Simultaneously and strangely, there was a tinge of shame and guilt at the realization that the attackers were of the same race as mine. And then I was overcome with a dark foreboding of "What's going to happen now to everyone who is Japanese?" I felt a despondent concern over innocent Japanese like my parents. My overall lasting emotion was a feeling of "I'm going to get you bastards for this!" I made a vow to fight them to my last breath. At no time while witnessing the attack was there a shred of doubt that Japan was now my bitter enemy and that I was a full, loyal American dedicated to fight and defeat every enemy of my country.

The University ROTC

While the radio announcer was calling all soldiers and sailors to return to their stations, I suddenly heard, "All university ROTC cadets, report to the campus immediately!" I immediately aroused from my stupor, got into my ROTC uniform and rushed up to the ROTC armory on the university campus. I was in my ROTC uniform within the first hour of the attack, the first of five uniforms I would wear throughout the next four years of the war.

I reached the armory around 9:30 a.m. and met other ROTC cadets who were arriving in response to the call. There was no formal signup or registration, no questions asked, no swearing in or any other formalities. We were not asked if we were Japanese nor was there any other sign of doubt or distrust. We were no different from any other American soldier or sailor reporting for duty in time of crisis. At full strength, the UH ROTC must have been around five hundred cadets, and fully seventy-five percent were of Japanese ancestry. We reported directly to our units. My company, Company B, had one hundred forty men, mostly freshmen and sophomores. Some of the familiar names in Company B were: Yoshiaki Fujitani, Claude Takekawa, Harry Tanaka, Akira Hamaguchi, Goro Arakawa, George Goto, Edwin Honda, Henry Kawasaki, Don Shimazu,

Richard Chinen and Warren Higa.

We were greeted by the sight of Sergeants Hogan and Ward feverishly inserting firing pins into our 1905 Springfield .03 bolt-action rifles. I found out later the ROTC staff had to make a frantic call to high school ROTC units for more Springfield rifles to fully equip our unit. Each of us was issued a clip with five bullets. I do not recall ever being issued more than five bullets. We had never been trained to fire those rifles. Nonetheless, we had responded to our country's call in the moment of peril.

Almost immediately we received our first order. It was to cross Mānoa Stream next to the campus to establish a line of defense across the foot of St. Louis Heights. Reportedly Japanese paratroopers had landed atop St. Louis Heights, and our orders were to meet the enemy and repel their advance to the city. We crouched down among the *haole koa* in the area that is now Kanewai Park, anxiously waiting for about five hours in the hot sun for the enemy. At first, to put it bluntly, we were scared shitless. But as the day wore on and we thought of the sneak attack that morning, another wave of anger consumed us. We resolved it was going to be them or us. Fortunately for us, the enemy never showed up. The Japanese paratroopers were just one of many hysterical rumors that spread like wildfire across Honolulu that day! However, for our valiant defense in "the Battle of St. Louis Heights," the Army in 1977 was to award the university ROTC a battle streamer as "the first and only ROTC unit in the United States to engage in combat action during World War II."

For those first few hours the UH ROTC had no official military status or standing, federal or territorial. We were just college ROTC boys responding to our country's call to arms. Little did we realize then that responding to that urgent call to duty, a UH ROTC regiment comprised mostly of Japanese Americans would set into motion a chain of events that led to a reopened opportunity for Nisei to fight for the country. I believe our story all started that morning of the Pearl Harbor attack. The University of Hawai'i and its ROTC unit should be proud of this contribution to the war, and I am certainly most proud that I was able to be a part of it.

The Hawai'i Territorial Guard

The UH ROTC had been on active duty for only six or seven hours on December 7 when the military governor ordered the unit converted into the Hawai'i Territorial Guard (HTG). We were trucked down from the university campus to HTG headquarters at the Honolulu Armory, where the state capitol stands today. Again, about three fourths were of Japanese ancestry, and no questions were asked, nor issues raised, when we reported for duty.

The HTG had three rifle companies of about one hundred fifty men each. We were dispersed all over the island, even as far out as Kahuku on the northern tip of O'ahu. The same organizational structure and rank we held in the ROTC carried over into the HTG, so I was first sergeant of Company B.

We were issued the round tin helmets of World War I vintage along with a gas mask. We were immediately assigned to guard 'Iolani Palace, the governor's residence, the courthouse, Hawaiian Electric Company, Mutual Telephone Company, the Board of Water Supply and other utility installations throughout the city, as well as other government buildings. Many years later Wilmer Morris, a university sophomore and ROTC corporal, told us how he had been assigned to guard the dynamite shack in the Mō'ili'ili Rock Quarry now occupied by UH. The sergeant of the guard forgot to relieve him, so he faithfully stood a lonely guard for several days and nights without sleep, food or water. Meanwhile, a nearby Japanese farmer offered him food and water, but Wilmer refused it. He was afraid he might be poisoned!

The night of the Pearl Harbor attack was the longest, darkest and wildest that I can recall. We lay down on the armory floor in full gear and uniform, physically and emotionally exhausted from the day's events, but sleep would not come. All kinds of emotions tumbled around inside of us. We still could not believe we had been attacked by Japan. A fearful concern as to what would happen to all of us of Japanese ancestry gnawed our insides. We realized everyone who was of Japanese ancestry was now on the spot. We resolved to prove ourselves as loyal Americans. Our immediate fear was that Japan would attack again at any time.

Outside, we heard nerve-wracking sounds of gunfire. Anything that moved or made sounds was fired at in the dark. There was complete panic and fear. The enemy was nowhere around, but a lot of pets and livestock were found dead all over the island the next morning. Around midnight an airplane flew low over the city and a machine gun atop the Board of Water Supply building nearby let loose with a barrage of fire. It turned out to be one of our own airplanes, but on that memorable night the modus of choice was to shoot first and ask questions later. Corporal Mun Kin Wong, assigned to patrol Ala Moana Beach, recalled that they heard a boat going back and forth in the dark offshore waters. One of his panicky boys fired his rifle at the boat, but it was a Coast Guard patrol boat, which angrily returned the fire!

In addition to the university ROTC cadets, the HTG accepted volunteers from the city, mostly local *blalas*. They were hurriedly sworn in, given khaki uniforms, a Springfield rifle and a crash instruction on sentry duty. First, if approached, they were to call "Halt!" three times followed by "Advance to be recognized." One of our brave lieutenants made his rounds in the dark of the night checking on his sentries. At one station he was challenged with three rapid commands to halt, followed by frantic rattling of the bolt action on the rifle. The officer yelled out, "Alright, soldier, what do you do next?" Out of the darkness came a panic-stricken voice saying, "Dis goddam gun no can shoot!" So thanks to the yet-to-be-revealed mystery of the safety lock, our young lieutenant was spared for future service.

Over the next few days our Company B was stationed at the Dole Pineapple Company warehouse on Iwilei Street and assigned to guard the gas refineries and oil storage depots, and also the canneries, factories and other vital installations of the Iwilei industrial area and Honolulu Harbor. I can still visualize the sight of our boys standing guard behind sandbagged barricades, peering out at the harbor waters, armed only with the puny Springfield rifles and five bullets. If the Japanese enemy had chosen to invade Honolulu, they could have waltzed in. Fortunately, the enemy never landed, nor were any bombs dropped on the industrial area. No matter, the important thing was we had responded, and we were proud to be in uniform and serving our country.

Our HTG service lasted only six weeks. After it became apparent that the Japanese enemy was far away and would not be invading Hawaiʻi, Company B was relieved from guard duty in the Iwilei industrial area and Honolulu Harbor, and we were trucked out to the Koko Head Rifle Range to be trained for the first time in how to use our rifles. We fired all day and got sore shoulders from rifle recoil, shooting from standing, kneeling and prone positions. At night we bivouacked in pup tents amid the koa bushes around the rifle range.

On January 19, 1942, we were suddenly awakened in the 3 a.m. darkness and assembled en masse. A tearful Captain Nolle Smith told us that orders had been received to release and discharge all HTG guardsmen of Japanese ancestry. If a bomb had been exploded in our midst it could not have been more devastating.

We were hit with the painful reality that we Japanese Americans were being rejected and disowned by our own country, just because we bore the face of the enemy. This crushing blow was, to us, far worse than the attack on Pearl Harbor. It never had occurred to us that our status and loyalty as Americans would be doubted or challenged. As I said, in my mind I was descended from Captain Miles Standish. We were shocked and angered that our country had been ruthlessly attacked by Japan but we were proud that we had been given guns to defend our country.

Suddenly we were declared suspect, unacceptable, unwanted and distrusted. To have our own country, in its most extreme time of danger and need, reject and repudiate our services was almost beyond comprehension, something more than we could take or endure. I once tried to verbalize my feelings of that moment. "Over sixty years have now passed since that day and I have had the benefit of a very good college and professional education in the meantime. But yet to this day, I have difficulty grasping words in the English language that can adequately and sufficiently describe our feelings that day when we Japanese Americans were dismissed from the service of our own country, only because our faces and our names resembled that of the enemy. There was no depth to which our emotions sank. The very bottom had dropped out of our existence!"

In the early morning darkness, we broke camp, loaded our things, and boarded trucks for the long, sad trip back to the University Armory to be discharged. This was a blow not only to Japanese Americans but to our fellow guardsmen who had stood side by side with us—guys we grew up with, played sports with, went to school with—who had absolutely no question about our loyalties nor any qualms about serving with us. When we were dismissed, those Hawaiian, Chinese, Korean and haole buddies, all cried. When our captain Nolle Smith gave us a parting message, he broke down, hardly able to finish. Of course, we cried too.

Varsity Victory Volunteers

We had nothing to do but to go back to the university, although a few found jobs in defense work. Education felt empty and meaningless. Neither books nor the classroom made sense, nothing made sense. Not when our country was crying for war manpower and military servicemen, and yet we Nisei were deemed useless, unwanted and distrusted. But shortly an event took place that would prove to be of vast historical significance.

One day late in January 1942, a dejected group of former HTG was sitting under a tree near Dean Hall on the UH campus when Hung Wai Ching walked over from Atherton House YMCA to talk to us. Hung Wai was a member of the key three-man Morale Committee of the martial law government, a highly influential position in wartime Hawai'i. There were about six or eight of us including myself, but I can't remember the names of who else was present. The ensuing dialogue to the best of my memory went something like this:

Hung Wai: "Sorry, boys, that was a real bum deal."

The War Years   37

The boys: (Sullen silence.)

Hung Wai: "Don't get too bitter now, they only did what they thought was for the best. They really don't know you boys like we do."

The boys: "No make excuse for them, Hung Wai. Tell 'em go screw themselves."

Hung Wai: "OK, OK. I know exactly how you feel. But what you going do about it? You going quit right here? You going sit on your ass for the rest of the war feeling sorry for yourself?"

The boys: (We are thinking, *Now he's going after our pride.*)

Hung Wai: "You think the only way you can serve is by carrying a gun? Sure, they don't trust you with guns but maybe they trust you with pick and shovel. They dying for defense manpower all over the island. You can be the man behind the gun. There're other ways you can serve your country. Why don't you guys volunteer for labor battalion work?"

The boys: (Incredulously,) "Labor battalion?" (Most of them came to UH to avoid a future of plantation work.)

Hung Wai: "Damn right, labor battalion!" (Shaking his bony finger at us.) "You think you too good to do labor work? Think of the drama! Here you guys at the prime of life and the intellectual cream of the crop. Yet you willing to give up your education and good defense jobs to go work with your bare hands for your country. What an impact!"

The boys: "Cream of the crop…shit!"

Hung Wai: "Sure, what can you lose? You already deep behind the eight ball since Pearl Harbor. Your honor is on the line. Here they take your guns away and kick you out of the HTG. You turn the other cheek. You go the second mile. You turn right around and say, 'OK, you don't want us to carry a gun, then find me your hardest and dirtiest work and I'll do it.' What a magnificent gesture!"

The boys: (Silent, still not convinced.)

Hung Wai: "Just think, you doing it for the Japanese. You the best ones to do it. You set the example for all loyal Japanese. They can't doubt your loyalty after that. They can't turn you down!"

Hung Wai was persuasive. He was artfully turning our focus from the gut level to appeal to our mind and hearts. It made good sense as he opened us to other options to be of service to our country while demonstrating our loyalty at the same time. We were finally convinced. John Young of the YMCA and the Japanese-American Emergency Service Committee got involved. Meetings were called to make the same appeal to other HTG discharges. Within several weeks, cynical and embittered minds were turned around. Dozens were now willing to offer themselves as members of a noncombat labor battalion.

Clearly Hung Wai's meeting with the boys established the idea and ideals that sparked the initiation of the Varsity Victory Volunteers (VVV). Hung Wai rightfully has been recognized and credited with being "the Father of the VVV." I like to playfully remind Reverend Yoshiaki Fujitani (of the Hongwanji Buddhist mission) that the tree where we met should be known as "the VVV Bodhi Tree," in reference to the original bodhi tree under which Gautama Buddha received enlightenment of the way!

The birth story of the VVV is covered in Dr. Franklin Odo's academic work, *No Sword To Bury: Japanese Americans in Hawai'i During World War II* (Temple University Press, 2004). Franklin recorded a long-forgotten fact that I was asked to make a first draft of a petition to the military governor. The final paragraph of that draft read:

"Our services have been sacrificed for the fulfillment of this goal but our loyalty remains untouched. We stand more resolved to defend with our lives, if necessary, this land of our birth, our homes, our education, our loved ones and our happiness, with much more vigor and determination than any imported defending force. We desire to contribute our share toward the defense of Hawaii. If our services are not required in the Territorial Guard, we wish to offer them to be used in any other phase of defense of our country."

Shigeo Yoshida, Hung Wai's close associate and also a member of the Morale Section, was asked to refine that initial draft into a simpler, more elegant final form. It read as follows:

"We, the undersigned, were members of the Hawaii Territorial Guard until its recent inactivation. We joined the Guard voluntarily with the hope that this was one way to serve our country in her time of need. Needless to say, we were deeply disappointed when we were told that our services in the Guard were no longer needed.

"Hawaii is our home; the United State, our country. We know but one loyalty and that is to the Stars and Stripes. We wish to do our part as loyal Americans in every way possible and we hereby offer ourselves for whatever service you may see fit to use us."

The petition was addressed to General Delos C. Emmons, military governor, and dated January 30, 1942. It was signed by one hundred sixty-nine Nisei, mostly from the university, who had been discharged from the HTG.

Would our petition be accepted? The total picture at the time looked dark and grim. The odds seemed stacked against us, considering the following:

1. Pearl Harbor was still in smoking ruins from Japan's attack.
2. The Japanese Army had overrun Southeast Asia and the southwestern Pacific Islands. Japan was expected to invade Midway and Hawai'i next.
3. Forty percent of Hawai'i's people were of Japanese ancestry; their loyalty was in question.

4. False rumors of Japanese disloyalty and treachery were rampant.
5. Not only had Nisei guardsmen in the HTG been discharged but some Nisei soldiers of the 298th (Federal Guard) Infantry had their guns taken away, and others were transferred to the noncombat Army engineers.
6. Navy Secretary Frank Knox was pressuring President Roosevelt to evacuate all Japanese from Hawai'i. Roosevelt instructed General Emmons to conduct a wholesale removal.
7. On February 19, 1942, President Roosevelt signed Executive Order 9066, which the Western Defense Commander, General John DeWitt, used to begin rounding up 110,000 people of Japanese ancestry in the western states into concentration camps.
8. The draft status of all Nisei was reclassified from 1-A (draft eligible) to 4-C (enemy alien).

Fortunately, rational thinking was the predominant response in Hawai'i. Against the rising national tide of prejudice and mistrust, military and government officials stood against the clamor to evacuate and intern Hawai'i's 160,000 Japanese. This was largely due to the intercession and support of local community leaders such as Charles R. Hemenway, Leslie Hicks, Miles Carey, Andrew Lind and Hung Wai Ching, who stuck their necks out and publicly expressed their faith and confidence in the basic loyalty and trustworthiness of Hawai'i's Japanese. What was needed from Hawai'i's Japanese at that time was not mere words and protestations but action—clear, bold, positive, concrete, demonstrative acts of loyalty.

The petition offered by the one hundred sixty-nine Nisei was just that. On February 23, 1942, General Emmons accepted our petition. The first volunteer all-Nisei unit of World War II, the Varsity Victory Volunteers, was born.

Franklin Odo's *No Sword To Bury* tells the VVV story against the setting of the Japanese immigration to Hawai'i, backed by detailed research and about forty personal interviews of VVV members. Franklin

My maternal grandparents, Taki (left) and Kinshiro Kagawa.

Top: Japan's consul general (seated, center) meets with my grandfather (top right) and others in 1909. *Above:* Grandfather Kagawa growing pineapples near Wahiawa.

My grandmother, Taki, and my mother, Yoshiko.

Top: *My father, Seinosuke Tsukiyama (top row, second from right), was a member of the Ginza Methodist Church in Tokyo.* ***Above:*** *My father (seated, fourth from left) gathers at an alumni association party in 1920 with his classmates from Japan's elite Keio University.*

My father in his student uniform in Japan.

Top: My father (top row, right) was an ardent supporter of the Ka'imukī Japanese Language School. *Above:* My mother attended a YWCA camp in Japan.

I was a "cowboy" at an early age.

Top: Tsukiyama siblings (left to right): Kazu, Martha, Jimmy and me. ***Above:*** *The neighborhood kids in 1926: Bobby Metcalf, Martha Tsukiyama, Donald Napier and me.*

quoted from the text of the speech I made representing the departing VVV volunteers at the university's aloha ceremony on the steps of Hawaiʻi Hall on the morning of February 25, 1942. With a mixture of pride and self-consciousness, I quote Franklin on my role in this work:

"Ted Tsukiyama emerged as the principal spokesperson of the university boys and of the VVV as a unit. His English Standard Roosevelt High School education was useful, and his Christian upbringing imbued him with a particular sense of mission. Tsukiyama was uniquely aware of the potentially momentous nature of the VVV. His private experience became the public model of VVV emotion, motivation, dedication, and success. In part, this was due to the peculiar usefulness of his individual case to the social construction of a Nisei myth; in part, it was his personal quest for meaning in a world turned hostile and vengeful..."

The cover of *No Sword To Bury* features one of the most famous photos of the VVV. It is of the boys sitting on the front steps of Hawaiʻi Hall on that day of the university sendoff. Another famous photo was taken of the boys lined up at ʻIolani Palace. Ralph Yempuku, our older mentor, was shaking hands with General Emmons just before we were loaded onto army trucks to take us to Schofield Barracks. We were designated the Corps of Engineers Auxiliary attached to the 34th Combat Engineer Regiment, but we soon were known throughout Hawaiʻi as the VVV.

When General Albert Lyman, head of the Army Corps of Engineers, was asked whether he would accept the Nisei volunteers, he reportedly said: "Gimme all those kids you got. I'll take care of them." The general surely lived up to his word. We were housed in regular army barracks in the 34th Engineers compound in upper Schofield off Kolekole Road. We ate army chow from mess halls, and we performed the same construction and defense work as the 34th Engineers. Yet we were uniquely a noncombat civilian component in the wartime army, with federal civil service status and all attendant perquisites. We were paid a salary equivalent to an army private.

The groundwork for the formation of the VVV assured that we would be led by sympathetic, understanding locals, not redneck

Mainland haole officers. Our commander was Captain Richard Lum. He was supported by 1st Lieutenant Frank Judd, executive officer; Lieutenant Tommy Kaulukukui, specially commissioned to serve as morale and recreation officer; and two Hawaiians, Master Sergeants Bill Jarrett and George Aikau, who served as clerical and supply personnel.

Hung Wai Ching wanted to have the civilian leader of the VVV be an older, more mature Nisei so, in consultation with Mr. Hemenway, Ralph Yempuku was asked to serve as our supervisor. At first Ralph hesitated because he was "still pissed off about being fired from the HTG." Mr. Hemenway encouraged him to take on this crucial role, and Ralph accepted. No better choice could have been made. Not enough can be said about Ralph's great leadership in keeping those one hundred sixty-nine diverse "characters" in the VVV focused and motivated. The VVV mission might not have succeeded as well as it did without Ralph as its leader!

I can never understand how I got to be appointed assistant supervisor under Ralph over any number of boys who were upper classmen and who already held ROTC reserve commissions. I can only attribute it to Hung Wai, who had gotten to know me through the Atherton YMCA and felt he could best trust one of his "Y boys." Because Ralph did not miss a single day's work duty during the months of the VVV, I never had to relieve him, and I spent my career at the VVV as a truck driver.

Otherwise there was no rank. Everyone was a working private. Even commissioned ROTC officers did manual labor. We had ten gangs averaging sixteen or seventeen men each: the kitchen gang, quarry gang, three carpenter gangs, two construction gangs and three field or road gangs. The gang leaders were Richard Chinen, Junichi Buto, Kongo Kimura (later Masaichi Sagawa), Robert Kadowaki, Richard Yamamoto, Tadashi Ikeda, Sukeyoshi Kushi, Unkei Uchima, Harry Tanaka and Claude Takekawa. We were armed not with guns but with hammers and saws, picks, shovels and sledgehammers. The quarry gang operated the stone quarry up at Kolekole Pass. The carpenter crews built furniture, field iceboxes, even flytraps; they also blackout-proofed the Post Bowl and other Schofield buildings. The construction gangs built portable field huts and warehouses while the road gangs dug ammo pits, strung barbed wire, repaired bridges, dug drainage culverts and built auxiliary roads in the Waianae Mountains.

These tasks must have been the "shit jobs" of the 34th Engineers as I can't recall seeing any of the regular engineers doing this work except to supervise us. We Nisei were quickly accepted and absorbed into the 34th Engineer organization as they became impressed with our hard work, dedication and good behavior, and also the fact that we got along well socially.

At first there were two armed guards on our trucks riding out to the field jobs each day, whether to keep surveillance over us or to protect us, but soon neither was found necessary so they stopped coming. We worked under the supervision of civilian US engineers. They gave us no army uniforms so we designed a white formal shirt with VVV insignia for parades, etc., and a blue denim uniform for our daily work. At first they gave us a white armband with "VVV" marked in green lettering for identification purposes, possibly so we wouldn't get shot at as Jap infiltrators! Gradually we stopped wearing the ID armbands as word of our positive presence spread. We became a familiar sight at the Schofield Theater, PXs and around the entire post.

We had a three-person office staff. Years later, Captain Lum confessed that one of his main responsibilities was to monitor our personal conduct and report to upper brass regularly as a security measure, but apparently it must have soon become apparent that the VVV boys passed the test with flying colors. We worked hard at our jobs and returned to the barracks dead tired, and thus we made a favorable name and reputation for ourselves with the military as well as civilian leadership in town.

Of course we had our share of "goldbricks." Always the same guys volunteered to stay back to clean the barracks so that they could sleep the rest of the day. One of our fellow workers (who shall remain unnamed) would lean on his shovel and gaze out at the horizon so often we nicknamed him "Columbus." One particular kitchen crew would suddenly disappear when there was work to be done and was aptly known as "Houdini." But overall, we felt trusted, accepted, useful and productive, giving us a sense of satisfaction that we had done the right thing in volunteering for the VVV. We set a positive example of service to our country in wartime, boosting the morale and the standing of the Japanese people, and proving our loyalty to America.

For me, the VVV turned out to be the happiest and most rewarding experience during the war, and in fact of my whole life. Although as Odo points out, we were a highly diverse bunch of characters, one could easily sense the common purpose and dedication that bonded us. We worked for the good of the country, for our families and the Japanese community at large. From the kindred souls of the VVV, I made close and valuable friends who would last a lifetime: Kats Tomita, Shiro Amioka, Buddha Hamaguchi, Akira Otani, Herb Isonaga, Hossie Toyota, Claude Takekawa, Harry Tanaka and Yoshi Fujitani, to name a few. I never met a more positive, inspired and worthy group for the rest of the war. Truly they were a unique bunch of guys. Maybe Hung Wai was right. They were "the cream of the crop!"

The VVV boys occupied a special place in the eyes of Hung Wai, the Morale Section and the Japanese-American Emergency Service Committee. The ESC report for March 1942 lists the formation of the VVV as "one of its major accomplishments." They never missed an opportunity to showcase the VVV as the poster boys of Hawai'i's Japanese community. Generous publicity was lavished on the VVV boys as we lined up to buy war bonds, made numerous trips to donate blood to the blood bank or served as one of the sponsoring hosts to the Wisconsin Day Luau, in appreciation of Wisconsin's fine treatment of the 100th Battalion at Camp McCoy.

Hung Wai Ching and the Morale Section sent us out to talk to schools and community groups to boost morale and to be role models of service to our country at war. For example, Shiro Amioka spoke to McKinley students. Harry Tanaka and I talked to plantation groups.

The origins of my public writing and speaking date to the VVV. We were required to write out our statements and to submit them for security and other forms of clearance. At the same time, I abhorred simply reading a speech, so I worked on sounding as if I were speaking from the heart or "off the cuff." I recall one night being driven out to Waipahu by police captain Jack Burns to speak to the Japanese community in a blacked-out gymnasium. So at the VVV I personally witnessed and participated in Jack Burn's wartime support of the Japanese, which understandably accounts for the rock-solid political support given by Hawai'i's postwar Japanese community to Jack Burn's later candidacy and tenure as governor of Hawai'i.

While at Schofield, I also wrote an essay entitled "We Must Win the Peace," which reflects our early linking of serving the country with creating a better country in peacetime. I entered it into a UH essay contest, to no avail, but it nonetheless contributed to trying to think my thoughts through. During this period I began the practice of writing long letters not only to family and friends but to key community figures who figured in our service. One early letter, I remember, was to the president of the Chamber of Commerce, Leslie Hicks, thanking him for his call for fair treatment of the Japanese at a time when hysteria was at a high pitch.

All told, the VVV was a unique, unprecedented social experiment in the dynamics of race relations in a wartime environment. It stemmed the rising tide of hysteria, distrust and prejudice against Hawai'i's Japanese at a most critical and strategic time. But it also had great military significance, since it was watched closely by the military officials nationally and in Hawai'i. Hung Wai Ching saw to that.

One day in December 1942 the quarry gang looked up from their work at the Kolekole Pass rock crusher to find Assistant Secretary of War John J. McCloy himself escorted by Hung Wai on an inspection tour. Hung Wai explained to McCloy that these were Nisei college boys who had given up their education to render menial labor toward the country's defense effort as a show of loyalty to country.

The War Department must have been impressed. A few weeks later, in January 1943, the War Department announced the formation of an all-Nisei combat team. It changed the Nisei draft status from 4-C Enemy Alien back to 1-A Draft Eligible and issued a call for volunteers. This is what the VVV was waiting for. From the beginning, the boys knew that the VVV was only a stopgap measure and that its basic mission was to win back the right to military service, to fight and even die as the only way to convincingly prove loyalty to country.

With the formation of the 442nd Regimental Combat Team, the VVV had fulfilled its true purpose. We voted to disband, leaving it open for the boys to individually volunteer for the new Nisei combat team. In a letter written to Mother from the VVV dated January 27, 1943, I wrote that about seventy percent of the boys favored disbanding the VVV. I hinted that I would volunteer with these words: "Last night I wrote to Naoko explaining everything and the way I felt… how hard it was to leave so many nice things behind and how much I appreciated them now, how thankful I was to be able to receive so many of the finer things in life that I should in return be ready to give something up for these privileges…and while I wrote, it brought tears to my eyes."

I took photos of our final beer bust on the lawn of the VVV compound with the 34th Engineer working colleagues, who thought we were doing the right thing to go "regular army" and wished us well. On January 31, 1943, we were trucked down to 'Iolani Palace for formal inactivation ceremonies, which were conducted by the governor's office and military officials. We received congratulatory messages from Colonel Sexton of the 34th Engineers, UH president Gregg Sinclair, Charles Hemenway, Leslie Hicks and Captain Lum. We then were dismissed, becoming civilians again, free to volunteer for the proposed Japanese-American combat unit.

It is difficult for me as an insider to accurately assess the true influence and impact of the VVV experience on Hawai'i's total war experience, so I will defer to more objective sources to make such an assessment. The traditional perspective was expressed by Shigeo Yoshida in his classic VVV Memorial Service address "In Memoriam," as follows: "It was the VVV which marked the turning point in the treatment of the people of Japanese ancestry in this Territory and their acceptance by the rest of the community. What followed afterward—the record of the 100th, the formation of the 442nd and its history of hard-won battles, the less-publicized but equally important and impressive record of the interpreter groups, and the work of the civilians on the home front—was the natural result of the trend which was started in the early months of the war when a group of you men, who numbered at no time more than 170, demonstrated to a suspicious and skeptical community that the Americans of Japanese ancestry were every bit as American and every bit as loyal to this country and to her ideals as any other group of Americans..."

The VVV was the first Nisei volunteer unit of World War II, even preceding the formation of the famous 100th Battalion, and it was a material factor in the War Department's decision to form the famed 442nd Combat Team. The broad, overall contribution of the VVV to history was extravagantly extolled by Odo in *No Sword To Bury* thusly: "The VVV was the leading wedge of a strategy that culminated in two related but distinct transformations in post-World War II America. The first was the establishment of a radically new multicultural democracy in Hawaii, liberated from the stranglehold of an entrenched white oligarchy. The second was the incorporation of Japanese American 'success' into what has since become widely known as the 'model minority' thesis" (Odo 2–3).

The final assessment of the VVV may have been best expressed by my friend Yuriko Shimokawa Tsunehiro when she wrote: "More important than anything else, however, was the pride they restored in us after the shame we were forced to endure. They gave us our first step in our claim to first class citizenship that had been denied us, and now we could hold our heads up high" (Odo 273).

The VVV was a sort of redemption for me personally. It resurrected me and my fellows from the ignominy of being rejected by the HTG. I cannot close this VVV narrative without paying tribute to the other one hundred sixty-eight VVV volunteers who dropped everything and magnificently answered the call. Six great heroes, Dan Betsui, Jenhatsu Chinen, Robert Murata, Grover Nakaji, Akio Nishkawa and Howard Urabe, volunteers for the 442nd RCT, never came back from the war. Their ultimate sacrifice won for us the good life we enjoy today.

The 442nd Regimental Combat Team

President Roosevelt announced the War Department's decision to form an all-Nisei combat team on January 30, 1943. He issued a call for Nisei volunteers with a famous exhortation, "Americanism is a matter of the mind and heart; Americanism is not, and never was, a matter of race or ancestry." These were timeless words drafted by Elmer Davis, head of the Office of War Information, not by Roosevelt. The War Department asked for fifteen hundred volunteers from Hawai'i, but the turnout in Hawai'i dwarfed that number. Hung Wai Ching and the Morale Division sent me to Hilo to recruit Big Island youth to volunteer. In this capacity I was one of the speakers at a patriotic rally at Mo'oheau Park by the bay in Hilo.

When the call for Mainland volunteers barely reached a thousand volunteers, the Hawai'i quota was increased to twenty-five hundred volunteers. Within a few days, the Hawai'i draft boards were swamped with almost ten thousand Nisei volunteers! Only one out of every four who volunteered could be accepted, and I was overjoyed to be one of them. I learned later that Hung Wai Ching and our other influential friends saw to it that those from the VVV were accorded priority in the selection process, and ultimately one hundred ten VVV were accepted for combat team service.

Those not accepted were crushed. One of the most poignant scenes of my wartime memory was looking into the despondent tear-stained faces of those left behind as our truckload of volunteers pulled out of the Ka'imukī Draft Board headed for Schofield Barracks. Unforgettable is the one guy who ran alongside beating his fists into the side of our moving truck shouting anguished profanities against the Draft Board and all whom he felt had denied him the chance to serve his country.

Once at Schofield I was assigned to Provisional Company Five, which combined volunteers from the Ka'imukī and 'Aiea Draft Boards. Company Five was to remain intact until we reached Camp Shelby a month or so later. My father's diary shows I was inducted on March 24, 1943. I received my dog tags stamped with Army Serial Number 30104628 and blood type A. We were all inducted as lowly buck privates. I remember being housed in tents (hence the name "Tent City"), sleeping on canvas cots, and being issued ill-fitting uniforms—the average Nisei was way below the average GI sizes. We were given a canvas duffel bag that was to house our worldly possessions for the rest of the war. I remember the medical exams and endless inoculations. I especially remember the guy in front of me when we were to bend over for an anal exam. "Spread your cheeks," the doctor said. The new soldier pulled his facial cheeks apart with both hands, baring his teeth!

At first there was no formal training except for close order drills, which was duck soup for those of us with years of ROTC training. On off hours, crap games were rampant. When all twenty-five hundred volunteers had assembled at Schofield, we were put on railroad boxcars on March 28, 1943, and transported down through Kipapa Gulch to Oʻahu Railway Depot, where we marched along King Street to ʻIolani Palace for an official sendoff, which was witnessed by the largest crowd to ever gather there. Unquestionably, we were heroes of the whole community.

On April 4, 1943, we were taken by train to the Iwilei railroad station, this time with our duffel bags for embarkment overseas. Troop movements were supposed to be classified, but word got out that "the boys were leaving." Both sides of Queen Street, from Iwilei to Pier 10, were crammed with families and well-wishers. In stark contrast to those poor kotonk volunteers who had to sneak out in the dark of night to enlist, we Hawaiʻi volunteers were accorded a hero's send-off.

However, our march along the three-quarter mile route was anything but glorious, because each of us was staggering under the weight of our duffel bags. Many of the boys had to be helped by stronger comrades or dropped their bags on the street in sheer fatigue. Dan Inouye in his book *Journey to Washington* excoriated the Army for not having the decency to take all the duffel bags by truck to the ship, allowing the boys to at least look soldierly as we marched. I completely agree with Dan.

No one was allowed on the pier as we boarded the troopship S.S. but I do remember seeing the sole figure of Hung Wai Ching down on the dock, seeing the boat off. The *Lurline* sailed out of Honolulu

Harbor in lonely stealth. On board, we may have had KP and guard duty (submarine watch). Otherwise the voyage across the Pacific was uneventful, except for initial seasickness for many on their first boat ride and, as can be imagined, crap games. Thousands of dollars of *senbetsu* (farewell gift money) changed hands. It took us only five days to reach San Francisco. I clearly remember the morning of April 9, 1943, when the *Lurline* pulled into San Francisco harbor. One of the guys way up near the prow looked down at the docks in utter disbelief, did a double-take, then turned to the others yelling, "Hey, come look the haole stevedore!" The *Lurline* nearly capsized as everyone rushed to the railing to see a haole doing stevedore work, a sight never seen in Hawai'i. The educational process for us naïve islanders had just begun.

We had another surprise as we looked down on the dock to see the familiar figure of Hung Wai, there to welcome us to Mainland America and to assure our safe arrival en route to Camp Shelby. Hung Wai later told us he then went to visit (the infamous) General DeWitt, head of the Western Defense Command, and that DeWitt was infuriated that this Chinaman knew all about the troop movement of the Hawai'i volunteers. Hung Wai said he asked DeWitt if all twenty-five hundred of us could be given a pass to Chinatown to enjoy a chop suey meal, at which point DeWitt seemed to think Hung Wai was plain crazy. Instead the contingent was ferried across the bay to Oakland to board cross-country trains. As we moved from ferry to train, we had to pass through lines of armed soldiers on both sides of our march, whether to protect us or to prevent us Japs from escaping, I don't know. We spent almost a week on the train from Oakland over the Rocky Mountains to Chicago and then down to Hattiesburg, Mississippi.

I distinctly remember that when our troop train finally pulled into Hattiesburg around April 13, 1943, there standing on the train platform waiting to welcome us to the South was the incomparable, amazing Hung Wai Ching! We later learned that while our train moved from San Francisco to Hattiesburg, Hung Wai had flown to Washington, D.C. He attempted to persuade the Army to move the training site of the 442nd out of the South to a more socially receptive environment. His request was denied, but he was allowed to go to Camp Shelby to assure that the Hawai'i 442nd volunteers would be treated well and their training would proceed smoothly.

Unfortunately, even the great Hung Wai could not have prevented the Army's decision to round up unwanted kotonk Nisei soldiers in February 1943 and send them to Shelby to be trained as the noncommissioned cadre. It fell to them to train the incoming 442nd volunteers, most of whom were from Hawai'i. I was present to witness the unforgettable scene when Shiro Amioka (who was one of Hung Wai's pets) ran into Hung Wai at Camp Shelby. Shiro didn't even bother to extend Hung Wai a warm greeting. Instead he went storming up to Hung Wai with "Goddammit, Hung Wai, how come the kotonks get all the stripes and us guys stay buck privates!" Poor Hung Wai, who otherwise walks on water, was being blamed for a Pentagon blunder. It contributed to the infamous buddhahead/kotonk strife that, in the view of Dan Inouye among others, threatened 442nd RCT unity the first few months of basic training. I found most of the draftee kotonks who were supposed to train us to be (in the words of one of my letters home) "aloof and condescending, showing a selfish 'get ahead' attitude at anyone's expense, sticking only to themselves, not understanding why we volunteered and not having the fighting drive and spirit that we had." I felt they had broken with the fine morale and spirit we brought with us from Hawai'i, and I wished instead that the Army had assigned the 100th Battalion draftee boys from Hawai'i to train us! Fortunately, we had a few kotonk sergeants like Jim Mizuno, Sam Ikeda and Toru Hirano who were "nice guys" and made our training a little easier.

At any rate, you can see this was an issue beyond even the power of Hung Wai to pull strings. He did visit the Hattiesburg police chief to assure him that these boys were American soldiers, not Japs, who had come to serve their country and were not to be hassled by his cops. Hung Wai took the same message to the editor of the Hattiesburg American newspaper and thereafter its "Japs not welcome" editorials ceased.

While in training camp, I resumed writing long and detailed letters about our experiences, our attitudes and our hopes for the future. This was partly out of a sense of mission and partly out of frustration with military life and the senselessness of war itself. Corresponding with people was a way out of emotional isolation, and I eagerly looked forward to mail call. Various people, notably Mr. Hemenway and Hung Wai Ching, kept my letters and eventually they were returned to me, providing raw data for my unfolding story.

The 522nd Field Artillery Battalion

On or around April 20, 1943, I was assigned to Battery B of the 522nd Field Artillery Battalion. This was a classic case of putting a square peg in a round hole, because the artillery needed people with arithmetic and technical competence, which I did not possess. For a while I thought about asking for a transfer back to the infantry, where I might better use the five years of ROTC training that was so clearly indicated in my personnel record.

I complained about this ill-suited assignment in my letters home, as well as other things, reflecting the fact that while I urgently wanted to serve I was not enamored with army life. I complained about taking time off training to perform "chicken-shit details" beyond guard duty and KP, like shoveling gravel, delivering coal to the huts in the battalion, and—worst of all—pulling the filthy stinking "honey wagon" detail. I questioned whether pumping out all of the latrines was making me a better soldier.

I was relegated to the lowly rank of buck private. I had started as a corporal in my ROTC training, risen to first sergeant, and was just six months away from becoming a commissioned officer. Thereafter I was first sergeant in HTG, then assistant supervisor in the VVV. After starting over as a private (one stripe), I was never to be ranked higher than buck sergeant (three stripes) in my entire three years in the Army! As these little blows fell, I forced myself to accept the "demotion."

More fundamentally, I was troubled by the arbitrary and dehumanizing nature of army life. I was thrown into a kind of debate with myself, in which I argued the obligation to serve against the high-handed aspects of the service. My internal conflict was reflected in my May 25, 1943, letter home, in which I examined the question of why one put up with "seemingly foolish routines, formalities and regulations" to serve. I concluded I was a sucker—"a sucker for this thing called democracy which is the fairest and the most just way of life yet known which has nurtured and protected you and me…it's time that we acknowledge our indebtedness." Some of my issues with the arbitrary nature of army life continued throughout the war, but in the bigger picture I was always a sucker for democracy.

At Camp Shelby, I trained to become gunnery corporal on Gun No. 2, a 105 mm howitzer cannon, in Battery B. This entailed receiving the firing data over the radio from the Fire Direction Crew and dialing the horizontal azimuth reading into the gun sight while raising or lowering the shooting angle on the elevation wheel crank. Meantime, a 105 mm shell was loaded into the gun breech, then the gun was fired upon signal by the No. 1 gunner pulling the lanyard. The gun crew endured the roar of the cannon without ear protection, leaving most of the 522nd gun crews with hearing impairments to this day. Unbeknownst to me, in combat the No. 2 gun of Battery B became the "registering gun" for the entire artillery battalion, meaning it was the gun that initially fired smoke shells until the target was calibrated and zeroed in. When the correct direction and distance to target was set, this firing data was communicated to the other guns in the battalion (four guns in each battery, three batteries in the battalion). All would then commence firing on the target upon the command: "Fire for effect!" So the gunner corporal on the No. 2 Gun of Battery B performed a key and heavy responsibility. According to Don Shimazu, the 522nd Field Artillery Battalion later earned the reputation overseas of being one of the fastest and most accurate among the artillery units in the European Theater.

When not training on the gun, the gun sections went out on combat-simulated field trips, convoys, maneuvers and marksmanship practice. We watched educational and training films, and we also went through physical conditioning, though not as rigorous as what the infantry troops endured. In fact the artillery had it much easier than the infantry because we were motorized and pulled our cannons everywhere with two-and-a-half-ton trucks. I vividly remember that on field exercises, the infantry was out marching on the roads by 7 a.m., whereas the artillery would leisurely board the trucks around 9 a.m. and roar past the infantrymen who trudged along the roadside, covering them with dust. I would duck down in the truck to hide from my infantry friends, hoping to avoid their derisive hoots!

My letters home say there were eighteen men assigned to our hutment, which must have included my battery mates Toshio "Bulldog" Nishizawa, Larry "Donkey" Nakahara, Rocky Tanna, Ed Nakamura, Edwin Honda, Kats Miho, George Muramaru, Dunn Yamauchi, Flint Yonashiro and Jeep Kobashigawa.

I personally had no problem getting along with the kotonk battery mates. I did not experience confrontations along buddhahead/kotonk lines that became legendary in other units in the regiment. However, I did have the misfortune of having one chicken-shit kotonk sergeant who acted the "tough guy" role and barked and snarled his orders to us like the proverbial marine training sergeant. He always seemed to pick on small guys like Eddie Honda and myself, never the big guys like Bulldog Nishizawa, whom he never dared to approach. Because of him, we would end up with the crappy assignments like the honey wagon. His identity will remain only as "Ike." He was the only kotonk who I can never forget. I really hated his guts, even to this day.

In contrast, I sorely missed the camaraderie of my old VVV gang, Herbie Isonaga, Kats Tomita, Shiro Amioka, Buddha Hamaguchi and others, who were in other infantry units. Every chance we got we would arrange to meet at the PX or USO after the day's training. Once in July we hired and split the cost of a taxi to take us to New Orleans for a memorable two-day pass. I took numerous photos that can be found pasted in my old photo albums.

One leave I will never forget was a visit to a concentration camp. One of the kotonk guys asked me if I would like to go with him to the Rohwer Relocation Camp in Arkansas when he went back to visit his parents, who were detained there. This involved a five- to six-hour bus ride up the state of Mississippi to Jackson and then crossing the great river to Arkansas. In the evening, we reached Rohwer, where I experienced a sight I was not prepared to see. We came upon a vast encampment surrounded with barbed wire, protected by guard towers with guns pointed inward. We were admitted past the gates manned by soldiers and given passes only after rigorous scrutiny (we, who were wearing the uniform of the United States Army!). Inside the fence we found barracks-like buildings housing thousands of Japanese people young and old alike confined within the enclosure. The shocking realization hit us, that all these people were really prisoners in their own country. They had been imprisoned by their own government only because they were Japanese!

This was an appalling situation that we from Hawai'i were totally unaware of. But then it was the general attitude and demeanor of those interned people that was most disappointing and demoralizing of all. Many of them, mostly the young men, looked at us Nisei in uniform with what appeared to be disdain, hostility and contempt, like we were stupid for having volunteered for the army. Everywhere we went in camp we were not welcomed, certainly not warmly, except for the girl USO group that entertained us. Otherwise, we were totally ignored. The general feeling was one of unconcealed bitterness. What shocked me the most was to witness a big *Bon odori* (traditional dance) being conducted that night out in an open field. There were hundreds of people, young and old, dressed in *kimono* and *yukata* with Japanese odori music and drums blaring out into the night air over loudspeakers, in open defiance to all who could see and hear. Coming from Hawai'i where all Japanese were urged to "act American, speak American, dress American" at all times, an open Bon odori was a rebellious-seeming act while our nation was at war with Japan. It struck me as being almost disloyal and treasonous. I was sickened by the whole experience and couldn't wait to get out of there, which I did the very next morning.

I conveyed my negative views in letters to Dr. Andrew Lind of the UH Sociology Department, among others. These were eventually quoted at length in a scholarly article he wrote for his department's publication "Social Process." He spared me by not revealing my identity. Today I re-read those words and feel ashamed at such a display of insensitivity and immaturity. I failed to see that Mainland Japanese Americans were the victims of decades of sociocultural prejudice and discrimination of an intensity unknown to us who lived in the more tolerant, sheltered existence of Hawai'i.

I cannot blame those people for being bitter, after what our government had done to them, after uprooting them from their homes and imprisoning them. I have often reflected whether I would have so gladly rushed to volunteer for military service as I did in March 1943 if the government had taken everything away from us and shipped our families off to be imprisoned in America's wastelands. The most dominant perspective on the bus trips to Rowher, and also to the Jerome, Arkansas, camps was Dan Inouye's book *Journey to Washington*. He relates that Hawaiian Nisei were awakened to the realization that despite the mass incarceration one thousand kotonk boys nevertheless had volunteered for the 442nd RCT. In Dan's account, this led to a newfound respect for kotonks and that thereafter the infamous buddhahead/kotonk tensions and encounters vanished. For myself, I wasn't there to see how these elements played out.

Military Intelligence Service

In July 1943, a recruiting team from Camp Savage Military Intelligence Service (MIS) school came to the 442nd Regiment's training camp. I was ordered to Regimental Headquarters to undergo an interview. Not wanting to be separated from my comrades in the 442, I put on an Oscar-winning performance of stupidity. I purposely flunked the Japanese reading and conversation tests, and I happily returned to my unit.

Several weeks later, we were undergoing firing exercises in the field. I was flawlessly going through my gunner corporal routine. I felt a tap on my shoulder and heard the terse order, "Return to the barracks and pack up your bags. You're going to Camp Savage!" I was stunned into a numbed stupor. I tried to dial the firing order I had just received. I ordered the gun fired, only to have the forward observer telephone back, "Hey, we can't trace where that shot went!" With the thought that I was being ripped away from the 442, I felt as if my whole world again had caved in.

Unbeknownst to us then, the Army put a higher priority on military intelligence training than on the combat infantry. The Army could, at will, go into any unit and select Nisei who possessed the competence, or at least the potential, to learn the Japanese language on a crash course basis. Fifty years later, at an MIS Reunion in Honolulu, Shig Kihara, assistant director of academics at MIS, revealed that he was the recruiter who came to Shelby in July 1943. I said, "So you're the sonnovabitch that railroaded me to Savage when I purposely flunked the interview!" Kihara laughed and said, "We knew when somebody was trying to lay eggs on us."

Two hundred fifty of us were recruited out of the 442nd and sent north to Camp Savage MISLS around August 20, 1943. We were assigned to Sections 28 through 42 of the MIS class scheduled to graduate in February 1944.

Those months at Savage were the loneliest and emptiest I have ever known. It was a severe test of my values. There was no feeling of *'ohana* or camaraderie among my contemporaries of the sort we enjoyed in the 442. In addition, I felt I was being deprived of the chance to fight "a real man's war" with guns in favor of a soft, safe job in the rear. This bothered my conscience for a long time.

I missed my close buddies. At one point Kats Tomita and Herbie Isonaga tried to transfer to Camp Savage, thinking we might be together again, but I discouraged them. I didn't want them to suffer through the demoralizing life of Camp Savage. Its training system fostered a pervasive spirit of competitive individualism. The students would fight and cut throat for grades and honors and promotional ranking, just like our Japanese school days. It was mostly a dog-eat-dog atmosphere of survival and self-aggrandizement, of self-preservation and self-gain. I wrote in my December 9, 1943, letter home: "We boys who have been in the VVV and know what cooperative living means are most disappointed...everyone complains all the time—some of these guys are really disgusting as far as attitude and manners go. There is no group spirit whatsoever."

I did admit, through my letters, that I had been decaying intellectually in the combat training at Camp Shelby, and that the scholastic regimen at Camp Savage forced me to activate my mental processes again. We attended classes and studied all day and into the night. Guys studied by flashlight after lights out or sat in the toilet studying under the only lights that were left on in camp. After four weeks of this, I was advanced two sections to Section 31, one of the higher sections. My letters home reflect that I kept my grades above ninety and was consistently rated high on the translation courses.

During our six-month crash course we were schooled in military intelligence against a Japanese enemy. At the time, we could not write about the curriculum but I remember that *heigo* (military Japanese) was the main course, along with translation into English, with instructions on the Japanese Army Order of Battle (organization), Japanese weapons, armament, aircraft and warship recognition and stuff like *shosho* (Japanese shorthand), all of it crammed down on a most intensive scale. I have never had to study so hard in my life, before or since! After five months, I recall laboring with the help of a dictionary to write a five-page letter in Japanese to my parents. My, they must have been shocked but very happy and proud! That letter is still in my war letters files.

Outside of our classroom study regimen, we were subjected to what I deemed was an unreasonably restrictive and chicken-shit discipline that any soldier undergoing military training would have to undergo. It was clearly not contributing to the building of effective military intelligence specialists.

My negativity regarding kotonks hit a high point at Camp Savage. I told my parents "these spiritless Mainland Nisei around here...they are the most selfish and complaining of them all...no wonder they were chased out of California. With their attitude, they will not settle their problems too well." To me, most kotonks were "individualistic and defensive, with a lukewarm sense of loyalty and Americanism."

My letters were replete with gripes directed against these Nisei. But with more time to reflect, I came to understand they were the way they were because of all they had experienced as a despised and distrusted minority in America, and that I too might have been as negative and embittered as they and might have never volunteered for service had I been so treated during the war. I guess my gripes became noticeably frequent, because I got a sharp lecture from my sister Naoko "to stop griping and shape up." I assured my folks that "I am determined to face and take the worst they have to offer but still come out on top. I still have courage enough to buck some of these insurmountable obstacles to reach my goal—'my head is bloodied but unbowed.'"

I resigned myself to this new twist in army life and tried to get over the idea that I was "shanghaied to Savage."

The most positive memory I have of my Military Intelligence Language School experience was being stationed in a far nicer environment. Minnesota was refreshingly different from Mississippi. The countryside was far cleaner and prettier. It got me out of the humid heat and impoverished living conditions of the South. It also got me away from the despicable segregation of and prejudice against the Negro.

The culture of the Minnesotans was so unlike the downtrodden people of Mississippi or the hateful haole of the West Coast. Minnesotans met and accepted people of Japanese ancestry without prejudice or bigotry. We were well accepted by the downtown merchants, the USOs and the local churches, where through Hossie Toyota we met a nice group of haole girls who welcomed Nisei GIs into their homes. We also met and were warmly accepted by families across the state border in Wisconsin. Once we rode a bus way up to Duluth, Minnesota, and the town of Superior on Lake Superior and several times down to La Crosse, Wisconsin. I could only surmise that the Northwest was largely populated by recent immigrant groups from Europe—Swedes, Norwegians, Poles and Germans who were "outside foreigners" a scant generation before. They well understood what it was like to feel and be on the outside of the circle of American society looking in. Our positive exposure to them helped to restore our faith in our country and its people.

After completing our language course in early 1944, we were released on a fourteen-day furlough. With Hossie Toyota and Clarence Hamaishi, I went all the way to the East Coast, visiting Boston, New York and Washington, D.C. I took numerous photos on my 35 mm camera. To say the least, a trip through the three big cities of the USA was most educational and fascinating for all of us. We experienced the cultural, financial and political centers of our great country for the first time. The greatest benefit may have been the complete mental rest I enjoyed on that trip. "I have seen the best in the nation," I wrote, "the heart of the nation, and now I'm satisfied. It was an entertaining, educational and enriching experience which no one will ever take from me nor one I can easily forget."

This was a poignant time in my correspondence with my parents. Other than my youngest sister Martha, they were alone. Jimmy was somewhere in war-torn Japan and I, with my training completed, was headed for an as yet unknown warzone. I shared with them my anguish over being separated from the 442, as well as my travels.

I often marveled at my dad's great letters, which were written in English that he first learned at a night school in Tokyo. I wished I could write in Japanese even half as well. Father was now fifty-four, which was older than that age suggests today. I wrote to him expressing my deep respect and admiration. I said I wished I could be half the man he was, and that he was a model and an inspiration.

To both my parents I acknowledged the warm and open hearts accorded to others and their influence and effect upon me. In my absence they had opened their home to such good friends as Kats and Herbie and also to other members of the unit on leave, high and low, regardless of social status. In appreciation I wrote, "You folks taught me one of the most important lessons of my life…equality and tolerance." I recalled when we went to church on Sunday evenings they would pick up old people and poor people from the piggery districts of Mōʻiliʻili to the slums of Kakaʻako. I used to dislike this because I felt the people weren't worthy. Now I realized such people were "rich in spirit" and from my parents' generosity I learned the Golden Rule, "Do unto others as you would have them do unto you."

Mercifully, we completed our crash course in Japanese military intelligence and graduated on March 24. I wound up celebrating it with a case of measles that broke out during the graduation ceremony. I ended up in the isolation ward of the hospital for a week. The hospitalization was beneficial, as I felt seven months of the intensive study pressure ooze out of me. I was ready for my overseas assignment and just dying to get out of Camp Savage.

About fifty or sixty of us MIS graduates were assigned to the Army Air Corps to perform signal intelligence, which is basically enemy radio intercept work. We were sent south to McDill Field in Florida for special training. We reached McDill Field around April 16, 1944. Almost immediately I landed in the hospital again, this time for a circumcision! McDill Field is like Hickam Field on Oʻahu, right on the ocean, reminding us of home. The Florida Gulf Coast is not Tobacco Road Deep South, but cleaner and with more of a middle class. The environment was more pleasant, except for the heat and dripping humidity. We were now Army Air Force, which was known as "the country club of the army." Our training schedule was lighter and easier than at Camp Savage.

We were trained in all aspects of intercepting enemy communications or "electronic eavesdropping," which would be conducted from safe, rear line installations, so that we were not exposed to translating, interpreting or POW interrogations under frontline combat conditions. Such an assignment could have been the biggest break I was ever to enjoy in my military service, but because of it I may have suffered twinges of conscience when I heard of my former comrades in the VVV being killed or wounded. I so reflected in my August 2, 1944, letter home: "It doesn't seem right that I who once looked after all of them is kept back here in comfort and security while they, the younger and less learned, must undergo the hardships of the front line, quake with horror at the whistling shell, and suffer the agonies of seeing close friends lying shattered and still. I am glad for my conscience' sake that we will be moving off soon."

At the end of our Florida training we were given a ten-day pass from August 5 to mid-month. I went to Washington, D.C. and New York City again, where I visited more sites and attractions and saw more friends, old schoolmates and fellow veterans. It was a great follow-up to my previous furlough. In Brooklyn I met Mieko Fuse (Takami), who my brother Jim was once enamored with, and then went on a double date with kotonk girls in Washington, D.C. arranged by Kazuo Yamane, who was working at the Pentagon. This date was a forerunner of what turned out to be one of the most significant twists of fate of my life. It was only a step away from how I was to meet my lifelong love.

We were assigned from McDill to the 6th Army Air Force Radio Squadron Mobile and moved out by train on August 16, 1944, headed to the West Coast en route to our overseas assignment. Our radio intelligence team was made up of twenty-five Nisei, twenty of whom were from Hawai'i. We were led by Staff Sergeant Sanji Shirai, a kotonk who had been sent as a child to Japan for education (*kibei*). This was so ironic, because kibei were often held in suspicion, but in our case his language skills were more authentic and therefore more useful than ours.

We were the first AJA soldiers to be allowed back in California, where we underwent our final training at Camp Pinedale, Fresno and Yosemite National Park. We got a lot of publicity and had a few ugly racist incidents with some redneck types in Fresno. We spent almost a week of field training at the beautiful Yosemite Park, camping out by icy cold streams. It was easily the most pleasant of my wartime experiences.

As we neared sailing into the unknown, my thoughts turned to the meaning of the war and to Hawai'i, which lay both literally and figuratively over the horizon. In a letter dated September 20, 1944, I wrote an essay titled "Our New Hawaii." I attempted to express the hopes, dreams and aspirations of us soldiers about the kind of home that would await our return. The basic message read like this: "The other day I stood on the shore near the Golden Gate and watched the warm Pacific come rolling in from the setting sun. It was the first time I had seen my home waters in 20 months and as I basked in the warmth and friendliness of the atmosphere, I felt closer than ever to my dear Hawaii."

I mused over the question: Are the people at home prepared to take the boys back? "Do they fully realize what the war has done to their hundreds of fighting men in mind, soul, and sometimes scarred and crippled body? No matter how young they were when they left, they will come home men. They will be changed, and they in turn expect certain changes in the life at home.

"They want to find a better place than they left. It will seem strange to them that they have learned so much if their community has remained dormant. For the first time, the soldiers were able to look back into their community and appraise it objectively, seeing shortcomings hitherto unseen. What's more, they have traveled the world and seen all the places they had studied and read about. They have made history themselves. They will have integrated all these impressions and experiences and formulated new ideas; they will go home naturally expecting improvements to be made in the life and attitudes of the community.

"Some of the less articulate can only say, 'When I get back, just don't let anyone question my loyalty!' But inside, they earnestly want to see something better for all that they went through—the heat, chiggers and fatigue of Mississippi; the loneliness, terror, bitter cold, sloshing rains and mud of the battles at Volturno, Anzio and Cassino. Surely something better must come out of those rows of crosses on some lonely Italian hill with names like Chinen, Tomita, Nagaji, and Betsui?

"And the more thoughtful and articulate will say, 'Hawaii is destined to play even a greater part in the future as the crossroads in the fast-developing Pacific civilization. She must groom herself for the task, the responsibility. Not only must she expand and broaden herself economically, industrially, and agriculturally to absorb the labor of her many hands, providing security in jobs, but she must bring about a great change in the social concepts of her diverse population.'"

I predicted that over time the people of Hawai'i would evolve into a new mixed race, "a neo-Hawaiian race" bringing together Caucasian, Polynesian and Asian strains. "Hawaii will not only be a social 'melting pot' but is destined to become a racial pot as well."

I predicted that the "reactionary, narrow, old-world attitudes of the first generation" would be discarded. Their determined clinging to old prejudices and customs, I contended, "has been the greatest factor of inertia and hindrance to the fuller Americanization of the youth of Hawaii."

"The petty prejudices against interracial mingling must go; the stronger objection against interracial marriages must be broken down. The racial 'ghettos' of our community must be diffused and reintegrated so that our social program will not be retarded by the presence of Li'l Tokyos, Chinatowns, Li'l Manilas and other such possible friction points and objects of criticism and distrust."

Six days after writing this, on September 26, 1944, our troop ship left the port of Wilmington, California, and headed west.

Shipping Out

Our troop ship was one of those Kaiser miracle ships of questionable seaworthy reputation, into which we were literally packed like sardines, housed in the deep, dark, tepid hold, sleeping four bunks high, forcing us to spend most of our trip up on the sunny and breezy deck. On the afternoon of September 30, the ship loudspeaker announced we were passing a hundred miles south of Hawaiʻi, which caused all the Hawaiʻi boys to flock to the rails sadly searching for the tips of Mauna Kea and Mauna Loa, each of us with thoughts of home. The ship stopped at Melbourne, Australia, for fueling and provisioning but we were not trusted to leave the ship.

We passed under the Australian continent, where we encountered a big storm. The ship crashed through forty-foot waves, shuddering and shaking as it smashed nose down, passing through wave after punishing wave. We were terrified, fearing the ship might break up in the frigid water. We clung to our bunks, puking all over the place. I have never wanted to ride a ship again! When finally we sailed into the Indian Ocean, it was warm and smooth as a mirror. After thirty-four days at sea, we pulled into Bombay, India, the point of debarkation into the China-India-Burma theater of the war. The date was October 29, 1944. Unbeknown to us, it was the same day as the last heroic charge of the 100/442nd that rescued the Lost Battalion of Texas soldiers in the Vosges Mountains of France.

Our folks back home did not know where we had landed, since our letters were heavily censored for the first time, with all reference or identification of India cut out. Secretly, I had hoped that our final destination would be India, and I was prepared to make the most of this experience. We were loaded onto a rickety Indian train and taken on a three-day journey across the Indian subcontinent to Calcutta, where we had a chance to view this totally strange and different countryside, communities and people along the way. I vividly remember one early morning around 3 a.m. when our train was stopped in a village. A funeral procession passed, accompanied by wailing flute, bells and drum music in an eerie, surreal scene like Arabian Nights come to life. It sent chills shivering up and down my spine. I realized just how far from home I was.

Reaching Calcutta, we were trucked to a US Army camp at Kanchapara on the banks of the vast Hooghly River, where we were housed in a tent city. We didn't have any technical training that I can remember, but we did have KP and guard duty. I recall well one time we were taken out to the countryside and required to patrol an old dirt road in the pitch darkness without even a flashlight. The jackals would engage in a chorus of terrifying howls from the nearby bushes, and I was never so scared in my life! I can't imagine who we were guarding against, since the Japanese were a thousand miles away in Burma.

We had a great deal of free time and went on pass to Calcutta several times, mostly sightseeing and occasionally gift shopping, absorbing the flavor of India. My most lasting impression was India's poverty, illiteracy, unbelievable filth and smells and the prevailing sense of the cheapness of human life. I saw four corpses up close in one day. I witnessed the open-air cremation of the dead at the native burning *ghats* (crematory) at the riverbanks.

College graduates could only hope for jobs as a store clerk. At one department store I put back an ivory carving in the showcase saying it was "too much," to which the clerk just blew me over with a line from Keats, "A thing of beauty is a joy forever." Would any clerk in a store in America give you an answer like that? You wonder how India can maintain itself as a democracy when opportunity is so limited, when only a small fraction of the population owns all the wealth and power.

My intense interest in India spurred my habit of reflection and writing to a new level. I carefully studied the journalist Edgar Snow's book *People On Our Side*, which covered India's geography, climate, economy, racial and ethnic populace, religions, political status and struggle for independence from Britain. I was also inspired by John Gunther's famous *Inside* series, which took a similar approach. I wrote a seven-page profile of India that I shared with my parents, who in turn shared it with the Japanese community newspaper *The Hawai'i Times*, which published my piece in both English and Japanese.

Now that I was overseas and feeling like a contributor to the war effort, my letters home were more positive in tone and spirit. My November 23, 1944, letter on Thanksgiving Day read: "(I feel) thankful to be alive, thankful that every one of you back home is well and happy, thankful that the war has not taken my closest friends, as yet. It is strange but I feel a greater freedom of mind and conscience, a greater feeling of ease and happiness than I have in all the months in the States training…it almost borders on a feeling of fatalism because I will have no regrets whatever happens."

I attended a Thanksgiving Day religious service in a chapel with a thatched roof, cement floor and rough mahogany benches. Accompanied by an organ, a Negro quartet sang in a rich, sonorous blend of voices, "Swing Low, Sweet Chariot" and "Nobody Knows the Troubles I've Seen." After a short message, the organ played "America" and a tall, pretty Red Cross girl got up in front and began to recite its verse. We were electrified. Home, family and country seemed not so far away after all.

As the prospect of facing the enemy approached, I found comfort in the simplicity of the place and the service. I decided that the problem of faith was the institutionalization of religion in churches, and that I had been put off by "the church built with all the weaknesses of mankind." I thanked my parents for letting me take religion at my own pace and for not attempting to force it on me. "That I am far from home," I wrote, "that I am seeing more of the world which we live in, gives me a better chance to find the creative power and spirit of life."

On December 16, 1944, the 6th Army Air Force Radio Squadron Mobile flew up to Ledo, Assam Province, in the northeast area of India (now part of Pakistan) to commence operations in an outpost on an old tea plantation in the town of Chabua. There the Nisei linguists were divided up into operating teams, listening to intercept radios around the clock, on the basis of four hours on and eight hours off. There were four intercept operators with an enemy radio frequency on each earphone, totaling twelve enemy radio transmissions. As soon as we heard live enemy traffic we flipped on the recorder, preserving the message on an old-fashioned wax cylinder. We did translations and called them in to our intelligence experts to analyze for flight activity and volume, number and type of aircraft and message content. Most of the enemy communication was in clear, un-coded voice, although each airfield had its own radio name and each fighter plane had a code name such as *Shiratori* (white bird), *Akabane* (red wing) or *Takawashi* (high eagle). They soon became our familiar radio voices, because the Japanese air operations had no idea they were being monitored by the Americans. We Nisei were only the ears and collectors of the raw intelligence. We did not know how the data was processed and used, only hoping that we were successfully contributing to the intelligence war against Japan.

My letters home were now free of griping. On Christmas Day 1944, we gathered, sang carols and listened to a brief message. It was a cold, cloudy days but inspirational. "And so Christmas, stripped of all its trimmings down to its simplest form, shows that it is a universal spirit and ideal," I wrote, "a feeling of faith, hope and brotherhood of man." To this I added, "The world and its people are bigger than we thought."

The privation of India's suffering masses was making me appreciate the relative privilege I had come from. With this upbeat thought, I was ready to go to the front. On January 25, 1945, after two months of operating against the enemy from Chabua, India, we were flown in to the strategic town of Myitkyina (pronounced "michinaa") to continue our radio intelligence operations from inside Burma.

The allies had captured Myitkyina from the Japanese five months earlier, in August 1944. This was the key battle of the Burma campaign. It gave our forces full control of the strategic Myitkyina airfield and opened up access to China over the Ledo-Burma Road. Despite the passage of time, Myitkyina was a scene of total destruction and devastation. Not a single structure was left standing. We were housed in a rudimentary tent city out in the field, where we had to cut the grass and dig drainage ditches around our tents. The smell of death still filled the air. Bleaching skeletons were to be found everywhere, attesting to the fierce battle. True to my craving to record, I captured these scenes on camera.

The Japanese forces were suffering from heavy casualties and severed supply lines and were being driven south and out of Burma. But they were still conducting fighter attacks from remote airfields, and they gave us lots of radio communication to intercept. After about three weeks of operations at Myitkyina, on February 12, 1945, we were trucked down the Burma Road through tortuous mountain passes and wild, intimidating jungle to Bhamo, where our unit was to operate for the next seven months, until the war's end.

On the banks of the famous Irrawaddy River, we set up a tent city named "Skinnerville," honoring our company commander, Captain Skinner. Our radio operations worked smoothly. In fact, our work seemed to get easier as Japan's forces were pushed south. Their aircraft flights became less frequent and their signals weaker. We made the most of our off time, exploring the countryside and getting to know its people.

My Burmese bearer (houseboy) used to take me hunting. We also visited the native villages up the river, particularly on native festival days and wedding days. We were warmly welcomed and entertained with Burmese feasts and *aye*, a drink stronger than *sake*. My photo album has recorded all of these scenes, including the bridal couples. There was one wedding, probably a matched marriage, where the bride was unwilling and cried throughout the ceremony. I photographed the dancers and musicians and other phases of native life in rural Burma. We strangers (who must have been quite a novelty) were accepted warmly and treated like honored guests everywhere.

In my day-off ramblings, I liked to go down to the Bhamo Bazaar, where the merchants sold sapphires and rubies. Actually this marketplace was off limits to American GIs, but I did not wear my GI uniform. I walked past the MP sentinel gate without ever being stopped. It was one of the times in my life it was an advantage to be Asian! I visited with the merchants, who I found to be warm and hospitable. They would talk to me about precious stones and also invited me to their homes for Chinese meals. I made friends with them, particularly an ethnic Chinese man who had become Burmese named Lee Chwan Peh, whose friendship I kept for many years through correspondence.

I learned about the famed ruby mines of Burma and the fabulous ruby city of Mogok, which was only a hundred or so miles south of Bhamo. I first tried to get there by jeep with Junichi Buto of OSS Detachment 101, a VVV friend. We took a direct route but were turned back forty miles short of Bhamo by bombed-out bridges. A second chance arose when eight of us from the unit including Captain Skinner were given six-day passes. The idea was to travel to the ruby city on a longer and more circuitous route. By then it was safe to travel more widely in northern Burma because the enemy had been driven out of the area. Censorship prevented disclosure of our route at the time, but I later filled in the blanks and traced our trip from Bhamo. We went over the tortuous Burma Road through high mountains to places of exotic beauty with exotic names; to the Namhkam Valley (home of a famous hospital) through Kutkai and Hsenwi to Lashio, then south down the old Burma Road toward Mandalay through Hsipaw and Kyaukme, then turning inland about fifty miles through mountainous tea country to Mogok.

We could only spend half a day there trading for gems with cash, cigarettes and other PX goods (including underwear), then headed for our home base. An overnight rainstorm marooned us, preventing us from fording two streams where the bridges had been bombed out by US pilots. We wearily reached home camp after two rigorous days of travel, often driving through the night.

I was gripped by the novelty, excitement and the sheer beauty of the mountains and jungles and all that I had seen and experienced in Burma. I sat down and wrote a summary sketch of a land and people that I had grown to love. It was titled "Burma Odyssey," which my parents also shared with *The Hawai'i Times*.

I recalled one scene as follows: "…we passed a big village under trees on the river bank about sundown and the crimson red reflection of the setting sun filtered flat thru the trees and etched our faces in a sharp glowing silhouette. We passed the village school where children's voices were singing the familiar (Japanese) nursery song 'Yuuyake Koyake' and I suddenly felt thrown back many years, just like I had known this scene many times. Something in those innocent voices, already seeming to have left the war far behind them, rang with the universal hope that we put in the generation of tomorrow to somehow make this a better world to live in than we did; something sad too, that our happy innocent days were long gone…and, unashamed, I let my eyes burn and swim with emotion because something soft and tender within had been touched."

My rich experiences in Burma expanded my horizons. I wanted to learn about the people and places of the entire earth. *On to China*, I thought, *Japan and Europe*. I wanted to see the aggregate beauty and explore the accumulated suffering. "I want to see it in all its truth and reality," I wrote, "for only then will I discover why I live and to what end. Knowing how the rest of the world lives, my own life will gain that much more purpose, and understanding and meaning."

March 25, 1945, marked the second anniversary of my army career, prompting sober reflection and self-appraisal. I looked back on my VVV experience, and my friends, with warm aloha. I looked at my Camp Savage experience with an undiluted distaste. I was grateful for being sent overseas.

Throughout the war I was concerned that my brother Jim, stuck in Japan when the war hit, might have been drafted into the Japanese Army, and I was willing to enter any Japanese POW camp to see if he might by chance be one of them. I also wanted a chance to confront any Japanese soldier, since I had vowed on the day of the December 7 attack that I would knock down the first Japanese soldier I met, smash his face and kick him in the balls. With all this as background, I was invited to inspect a Japanese POW camp. I entered the compound with my big chip on the shoulder, ready to wreak vengeance on the hated enemy. Instead of the arrogant human fighting machine our training orientation had taught us to expect, I was greeted by a pathetic, fearful, dispirited group of young rural kids. They had been conscripted into military service by Japan's desperate army. They faced defeat, shame and humiliation for being captured rather than dying honorably in battle. They expected to be killed after being interrogated.

Any impulse I had to physically punish the prisoners quickly vanished. This was not the despicable enemy we had been taught to fear and hate. My pent-up anger and malevolence against an enemy that had caused so much wartime suffering and tragedy drained out of me. I realized that these kids were victims of a war not of their own making. Our only true enemy remained the militaristic warlords such as Tojo who had plunged their own country into a military disaster and who were to meet their just fate at the war crimes trials to come.

I will never forget the monsoon rains of Burma. The rainy season started around May and lasted several months. By July, it rained almost daily, and at one time almost two weeks of continuous rain fell through day and night. The rains cooled off the stifling heat, but when the sun came out, a suffocating humidity enveloped us, at one time reaching a recorded temperature of one hundred and twenty-six degrees! The great Irrawaddy River, which drains all of upper Burma, overflowed its banks in no time and we had to move the Skinnerville camp up on higher grounds, right next to the Burma Road. There we spent many of our monsoon days under roof catching up on our reading and letter-writing.

As I look back at my Burma sojourn, I think I could not have been assigned to serve in a better place, with its savage geography, wild beauty and wonderful people. The Burmese welcomed easily and shared what little they had wholeheartedly. They were sincere and diligent, honest and trustworthy, unobtrusive but dependable, with a quiet dignity and modesty that did them great credit. I grew fonder of them as the days went by and would find it hard to leave Burma because of their warm friendship.

That long sought possibility arrived on August 6, 1945, when we heard the astounding news that America had dropped a new and devastating bomb on Japan, giving rise to hopes that it would soon lead to surrender. This was almost unbelievable, since we had expected at least another year before the war would end. We were on the road across the mountains in Namhkam Valley when the radio advised that a second destructive bomb had dropped, this one on Nagasaki, and that Japan was ready to accept the terms of the Potsdam Declaration.

My feelings upon hearing that the war was over were simply indescribable! There was no wild celebration, just a sense of immense relief as the mental and emotional burdens on the mind and soul lifted. We were all filled with an airy feeling of happiness. We immediately raced back over the mountains, reaching our Bhamo camp at 4 a.m. Because the Japs had been defeated in Burma, our unit had been poised to move to Kunming, China, but now our thoughts turned to how and when our unit could be disbanded and sent back to the US homeland.

I personally wanted to get out of the combat zone before the Army might decide to send me to Japan for occupation duty. As it turned out, we spent another five weeks in Burma breaking up our equipment (what a huge waste!) and just waiting. On September 16, 1945,

Top: At age five, I visited our ancestral village of Enoura in Shikoku, Japan.
Above: My senior photo in the Roosevelt High School yearbook.

Top: During World War II, Nisei were eager to serve their country.
Above: My greatest disappointment was being deprived of sharing the battlefield experience with my comrades in Europe.

Proudly wearing my dress uniform in training camp.

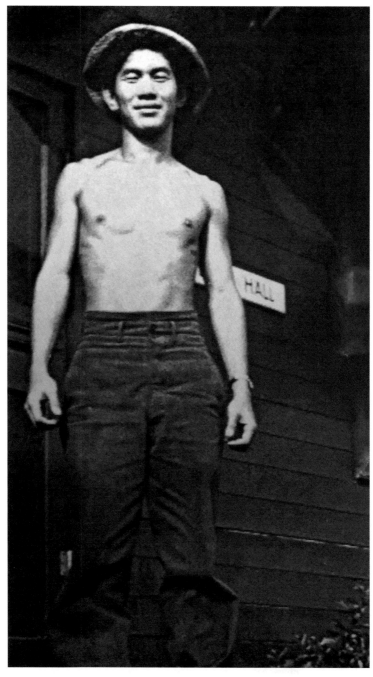

My life as a radioman and, opposite, with a friendly goat.

Top: *On leave at Coney Island in New York City.* ***Above:*** *My friends and I partying on leave before shipping overseas.*

Top: *Our Military Intelligence staff members pose with Burmese villagers.*
Above: *A Chinese bazaar in Burma.*

Posing with Kachin tribespeople, who were our allies in Burma.

when those of us with the most points (I had sixty-eight) were airlifted out of Burma back to our main camp in Calcutta. This was a month after the surrender. My letter home dated September 16, 1945, titled "Farewell Burma," began as follows: "It was a cloudy dismal morning with low sullen clouds hanging low over the horizon, threatening to break out in to rain any moment almost as if it might burst out into tears at our leaving. Our transport…flashed over the Ledo Road passing the edge of the strip and banked over the flattened remains of Bhamo. Down the road we recognized each turn, bridge and grade and turned our last gaze upon our white tents nestled upon the hill. We gain altitude and roared over the swollen Irrawaddy River and I searched for the Bhamo Bazaar where all my friends there were looking up, because I told them I would wave a handkerchief at them. I'm sure those friends really were looking up and wishing me a fond farewell…I touched my pocket to remember the trinkets and little presents that they showered upon me upon my departure. I felt myself growing heavy with sadness of leaving these people who took me into their hearts, this land that I grew to love so well…it was almost like leaving home again."

We were again housed at our unit headquarters at Camp Barrackpore, India, an ancient military post where we were to wait a seemingly interminable two months before we could board the transports for home. We sweltered in the humid heat waiting for shipping orders while boat after boat left India without us. If we had to wait so long, I would have much preferred to wait it out in Burma rather than in the squalor and stench of India. We killed time on passes to Calcutta, where we shopped (on limited funds), went sightseeing to historic places like the famed Black Hole of Calcutta and took a lot of photos. I even met and made friends with a high caste Brahmin girl named Dipali Ray, who was a niece of the Raja of Digapatiya in northern Bengal province. She graciously invited me to tea at their palatial home.

Finally, on November 11, 1945, we boarded the troop ship in Calcutta and set sail for the good old USA! Again, thousands of GIs were crammed into every available space on the ship, bunking three or four deep in the stifling, poorly ventilated holds. It was made even less tolerable because the war was over and we finally were going home! We were at sea for twenty-five days, enduring the heat of the Indian Ocean and Red Sea, stopping at the Suez Canal, then sailing on to the pleasant cool of the Mediterranean, past Gibraltar, then out into the frigid Atlantic, where we survived some huge storm waves and got sick as hell. We debarked at New York Harbor on December 6, 1945, completing my trip around the world, courtesy of the US Army.

We stood on deck in the icy wind at dawn as we passed the Statue of Liberty, gazing at that noble figure in awed emotional and tearful silence, warmed by the happy realization that this was the moment we had long dreamed of. Finally we were home from the wars! There were no bands or welcoming crowds to greet us but that night at Camp Kilmer, New Jersey, we were fed a great steak dinner and slept on a soft bed with clean sheets. There I ran into a big group of 442nd returning veterans including many of my old 522nd Artillery mates. We had a great reunion. I enjoyed a brief twelve-hour pass to New York City where I called upon a few friends and enjoyed a delicious Japanese meal at the Miyako Restaurant. In an amazingly short period of getting "demilitarized" at Camp Kilmer, we were put on a plane and flown to California on December 11, 1945. We rode for fourteen hours in an ancient C-47 cargo plane with only bucket seats, bundled in blankets and overcoats in an unheated plane in the dead of winter—one air trip I will never forget. We landed at the West Coast Debarkation Center of Camp Beale up in Marysville, California, where several thousand returning GIs were assembled for discharge, including hundreds of 442nd veterans. We were kept over a month at Camp Beale waiting for available shipping to Hawai'i, and then we were sent down to Camp Haan near Riverside a week after New Year's 1946.

There I was reunited with Kats Tomita, and we spent time on passes to Los Angeles visiting Hollywood and seeing friends like Phyllis Tam, the Metcalfs and the Eichelbergers. Finally around January 7, 1946, we were loaded on an ancient banana freighter, the

USS *Mexico*, to set sail for Hawai'i with a large contingent of returning 442 veterans. The happy voyage home was unremarkable, except a few days out of Hawai'i I came down with a high fever and chills and was put into the sick bay. The medics were unable to diagnose my illness, which turned out to be my first malarial attack. They shot me full of penicillin to curb my fever, which in a few days broke out into an itchy rash all over my body. In the next few days during my medical exam for discharge, I was given a ten percent disability rating for malarial infection, which later translated into a PL-16 status for the GI Bill. This was to completely pay for my next years of undergraduate and graduate education. So I always gratefully credit that one Burmese Anopheles mosquito for my GI Bill benefits.

We were met by a large welcoming crowd, band music and everything, a most fitting reception by Hawai'i's people in greeting their returning war heroes. After a few days of processing at Fort Armstrong, I received my discharge papers from the service on January 15, 1946. My days as a soldier in World War II were finally over. I was once again a happy civilian!

Postscript to War

What are my lasting impressions on my wartime experience?

Anyone who performed military service in World War II must inevitably and inescapably come to hate and be opposed to war as an instrument of national policy pursued by any nation. War can only bring tragic loss of life, vast waste of national resources and grievous human suffering. Because this war was forced on us by enemy attack, leaders of Axis nations rightfully deserved their ultimate punishment as war criminals.

I found military service to be an utterly demeaning and dehumanizing experience. Individualism and free thought become submerged in the name of discipline to "the good of the whole," that is of the army, for better or for worse, and I often found it to be the latter. More often than not the army did not make sense. It disregarded my five years of ROTC training, which qualified me for infantry duty. It first assigned me to artillery, for which I had no apparent aptitude. I then was shanghaied into military intelligence when my competence in Japanese was mediocre at best. The army indeed specialized in pushing square pegs into round holes.

Generally, I look upon my army career with disappointment and largely in the negative. The greatest disappointment, as I've said, was being taken out of the 442nd RCT Combat Team and being deprived of the challenge of fighting in the European battlefields. My ultimate military intelligence service was undistinguished, trivial and exiguous, merely stealing enemy signals from the safe and comfortable confines of the rear line areas. Of course, I won no medals nor awards and my lowly duties never justified a rank higher than three-stripe sergeant. When I compared myself and what little service I contributed as a soldier to that of my colleagues of the 100th Battalion and the 442nd Regimental Combat Team, and the bitter hardship, suffering, injuries and even the supreme sacrifice paid and endured by them, I felt I could only hang my head.

When viewed in the larger perspective of World War II, I am inclined to feel a little more salutary and rewarded, particularly when considering my part in the earliest phases of the war as a member of the UH ROTC, the HTG and the VVV. History will note that those few Nisei of the ROTC and HTG, numbering only several hundred, responded without hesitation to their country's call to arms when most needed in those first few terrifying weeks of the war, at the moment all Japanese were regarded with fear and distrust.

History has abundantly documented the significance of the VVV as the first concrete demonstration of the loyalty of Hawai'i's Nisei to country, as the first Nisei volunteer unit to be formed in the war, and as an instrumental factor in the War Department's decision to create an all-Nisei combat team. I am proud and gratified that I was an active ground-floor participant in all three of those little-known historic units of World War II. All in all, having worn the uniform of six different military and quasi-military units during the war, I can take comfort that I can be counted among those thousands of

Nisei who answered the call. Our service successfully turned the tide of fear, suspicion, doubt and prejudice against the Japanese, who convincingly demonstrated that Americanism is not a matter of race or ancestry but of the mind, heart and spirit. Loyal service and sacrifice made a better life and world for all people of Japanese ancestry who lived in Hawai'i and on the Mainland USA. ☛

Part Three

The Postwar Years

Back to School

My overriding concern at the war's end was to complete my education. I first had a little unwinding to do. For lack of athletic activity, I returned home thin and flabby. I was also afflicted by monthly attacks of malaria during this period. I hit the beaches swimming and bodysurfing and played tennis and golf at every chance. I visited my sister Naoko and my first nephew, Jon Ogata, on the island of Kaua'i. Then Herbie Isonaga and I visited the Big Island to meet friends and retired veterans all over that island. We called on one veteran from Herb's company who was running the family store on the Hamakua Coast. He was sitting in front of the store, bored stiff after an exciting 442 combat and travel experience. He was absolutely delighted when we drove up. He rushed to the back of the store to kill a chicken, preparing a meal befitting his honored guests.

I enrolled for the second semester at the University of Hawai'i starting in February 1946. When we returned to campus, it was full of veterans who had a difficult time hitting the books after a steady diet of comic books. These were the guys who sat under the trees, ogling and catcalling the coeds or reliving the more exciting and glamorous lives they had just left.

The hang-loose life was tempting. Almost weekly we had beach picnics and beer busts. All these good times came at the expense of studies we were supposed to be pursuing. It was then I realized I had to go away to finish college in a more serious educational environment. I resolved that I had better look to the Mainland to complete the college education I had so sorely missed while in the service. I had signed up for twelve credits of some tough courses in economics, history and government, but the greatest challenge was meeting and studying under a professor who was to literally change the course of my life, Dr. Allan F. Saunders.

I had never encountered someone like Dr. Saunders. His two courses, Administrative Law and the History and Government of the Soviet Union, were more than tough. He eschewed the insipid rote learning system of lecture and regurgitation. In its stead he employed a Socratic cross-examination. He never dispensed direct answers but instead subjected us to a merciless barrage of questioning on the subject at hand.

University of Hawai'i students had not previously undergone such an inquisitional instructional process. We were good at straight note-taking and memorization but were never exposed to thinking on our feet and answering, let alone arguing back at the professor. My answers to Professor Saunders' questions ranged from feeble to pathetically bad, but I didn't quit and withdraw. In him I found a rare teacher who was really interested in us students and wanted to help us learn. He graciously gave me an A and B for the semester, neither of which I deserved.

Allan Saunders had just joined the UH faculty in 1945, so I was fortunate to become one of the earliest beneficiaries of this remarkable pedagogue. He was to literally revolutionize the UH classroom and the faculty/student relationship for decades to come. He was a humanist. He was socially democratic. He was the first professor to invite Asian students to his office and even to his home for both discussion and social intercourse. He befriended and enriched hundreds of students over the course of his teaching career and became easily the most popular teacher at the UH campus.

Indiana University

Professor Saunders personally befriended me, and in the process he helped me relocate to a Mainland college. In 1946 it was difficult to get in any Mainland institution because of the flood of veterans, and there was no dormitory space for out-of-state students.

By a great stroke of fortune I was referred to Dr. Saunders' good friend, Dr. Oliver P. Field of Indiana University (IU). Dr. Field taught government courses, like Saunders, and was an eminent figure in administrative law. The IU Board of Regents was not ready to accept a student of Japanese ancestry, but Dr. Field interceded directly on my behalf with the university president. I was the only Japanese American in a student body of over fifteen thousand! Professor Field went on to serve as my unofficial guardian while at IU, welcoming me into his home many times. Professor Field was totally blind, but he nonetheless taught several courses in my pre-law major. He would tap his way up to the podium, put his cane on the desk and then proceed to deliver a full hour of lecture, all without notes.

IU was in the southern part of the state in Bloomington, which was way off the beaten track in South Indiana. Except for a few intra-university events like the Hoosier football games, symphonies, drama and noted lecturers, there was not much social activity to speak of, so I had lots of time to focus on my studies. This was much unlike my "fool around" days at UH. Professor Field, like Dr. Saunders, was generous with his grading, and overall I did well in my two semesters at Indiana, getting straight As except for one A-minus. I remember one dorm mate who remarked: "You dumb bastard, how come you made only A-minus!"

I was housed at Rogers Center, a cluster of wooden barracks hastily set up in what previously had been a cornfield about a mile from the campus. IU was a strong "Greek letter" campus before the veterans arrived, but my student universe was made up of veterans. Under the Greeks, you were a nobody until you were pledged into one of the many fraternities. The veterans disdained fraternity life and thereby evened up the scales. Non-Greeks began to win student government offices, breaking the Greeks' dominance over student politics.

I was the lone Asian and never encountered discriminatory or unpleasant treatment, but among the White Anglo-Saxon Protestants (WASPs), there was an obvious strong prejudice against the many

Jewish students who came from the East Coast. I made some good friends in the dorm, notably a Navy veteran named Chuck Rutherford, who was my roommate; Bill Snider, who invited me home during the holidays; and Herb Hoppe from Cleveland, whose family helped me get a summer job and opened up their home to me before I went to law school.

Once you let them get to know you, haole people on the Mainland can be the nicest people in the world, without a trace of any racial distinction or consciousness, treating you as one of them. Spending one year in mid-America while at Indiana University was a most gratifying educational experience in itself and exposed me to the better side of this great country. Like Wisconsin, it was in sharp contrast to the backward South I was exposed to in Mississippi.

While in Indiana I suffered several attacks of malarial fever, body aches and chills that I foolishly endured in silence (*gaman*), shivering under covers to keep warm instead of reporting to the dispensary. This was to cost me my ten percent disability rating for malaria because the Veterans Administration soon claimed that I had established no postwar medical record of malarial attacks. Fortunately, I had applied for and received a GI Bill (Public Law 16) status earlier in the year so I was able to receive educational costs and living allowances higher than the usual (Public Law 345) all the way through law school.

During the Christmas vacation of 1946, I toured the East Coast (including a visit to Bob Potter's home on the east shore of Maryland, where I had a bad malarial attack). I checked out the law schools at Pennsylvania, Columbia, Yale, Harvard and Michigan. I applied to all of them. These were the top five law schools of the time.

On graduation, Professor Field kindly wrote letters of recommendation to each of the schools. All five accepted me. That's how big and influential a man Dr. Oliver P. Field was, but it all started in Hawai'i with his good friend Dr. Allan F. Saunders.

I decided on Yale Law School. Between Indiana and starting Yale, I had to find a job in the summer of 1947 to sustain myself. I was hired by the Bay City YMCA as a camp counselor and tennis instructor at Sand Lake near Saginaw, Michigan. I spent a memorable summer with groups of young campers, including a great canoe trip down the famous Au Sable River. I traveled over to Wisconsin and Minnesota to visit wartime friends and then I was ready to enter law school.

Yale Law School

Admission to Yale fulfilled a long-nurtured aspiration that incubated before the war, when most Nisei youth could only envision or aspire to a career in teaching or business. I picked Yale over Michigan and Harvard because of its reputation as a progressive legal institution as well as its superb physical facilities. Weighing heavily in my decision was the faculty presence of Eugene V. Rostow, the first public figure with the guts, social conscience and civil rights advocacy during wartime to publicly speak out against the unconstitutionality of our governments' evacuation and imprisonment of Japanese Americans. The title of his Yale Law Journal article suggests the tone he struck: "The Japanese American Cases—A Disaster." I was to find out later that I was the first student of Japanese ancestry to enroll and to graduate from Yale Law.

I can never forget those first few weeks. I became immersed in a life of intensive study under brilliant law professors, surrounded by bright and articulate students who were much smarter than I. I never had to study so hard in my life, just to survive. I was in the books up to one o'clock most nights. I often wondered whether I had made a mistake in choosing law as a life profession!

In the midst of this I received news that our great wartime champion Charles R. Hemenway had passed away. I will always remember how fortunate and blessed we in Hawaiʻi were to have such a big, influential leader in the community come to the support and defense of Hawaiʻi's Japanese in those dark days of fear, distrust and hatred. He truly must be credited with being the most influential force in saving Hawaiʻi's people from the tragedy of mass evacuation and internment. He first was my mentor and then my friend. I will always treasure the encouraging personal letters that Mr. Hemenway, despite his busy work life, wrote to me, an insignificant nobody out in the wilds of India/Burma. He was one of the greatest men ever to live in Hawaiʻi.

Because of the challenging workload, much of those three years became a blur. I did write home extensively, and my folks were good enough to save a stack of my letters. My first courses were Contracts, Criminal Law, Procedure, Judicial Process and Legal Research. My October 27 letter home reported, "We have to read cases for each one of these courses and it is darn hard to understand them, much less keeping them straight. There are about 175 in our class and they are all undoubtedly the pick of the crop, all very intelligent, serious, matured and very well prepared to speak up and discuss problems in class. I cannot help but feel, despite one year at Indiana, how poorly prepared I am compared to most of them. U of Hawaii fails to teach its students to think for themselves, and to express their thoughts in class in an effective manner. Seeing the rest of them, it only makes me realize how much harder I have to try to make good here."

While the others might be aiming to run a four-minute mile, I resolved to run at my own pace and be happy to complete the three-year study at Yale. I had a single room on the third floor of the Sterling Law Building equipped with a big desk, with easy access to the law library, so that all life outside of class was focused on homework and study. Attending and studying at a top law school had its benefits. In my December 4 letter home I wrote: "As long as I can feel fascinated about the subjects and keep that eagerness to learn, studying long hours does not have its tiring or unpleasant aspects, so I will try to preserve that enthusiasm."

Even if I had the time, I couldn't have played around much, since the GI Bill ($105 per month) only covered the basics of tuition, room and board and nothing for extras. During breaks, I did run down to New York to visit Kats Tomita, Art Wong and others. I also had Hawaiʻi friends who came over during football weekends, such as the Yale-Harvard game, to break up the monastic habits of study. Life was made easier and more pleasant by the great classmates who befriended me, such as Jerry Katcher, Mel Shimm, Bill Shank, Jerry Preston, Charlie

Parker, Tom Stewart, Andy Wood, Irving Morris and others who had accepted me without reservation and become my lifelong friends.

After a tense February 1948 of taking our first-term exams, I received the results with great surprise—one A and five Bs for a 75.6 average, which was within the top twenty percent of the class. Being assured that I would not flunk out of law school, the second term of my first year went by uneventfully. Since I had not been home for two years, my folks must have sent me money to return to Hawaiʻi for the summer. I worked at Hung Wai Ching and Ruddy Tongg's coconut chip factory for a couple of months. I scouted around for future job prospects and went to some great beach picnics with the VVV gang and dates out at Makapuʻu Beach.

As a result of Hawaiʻi students studying on the Mainland, I was no longer so lonely for island company. On the way back to law school, I stopped for a few hours to visit Kenneth Chang in Chicago and stayed overnight with Art Wong and Kats Tomita in their new 3rd Avenue apartment. Art and Kats in turn visited me at Yale for the first time, coming up for the Yale-Dartmouth game and bringing Pearl Yim, Charlotte Wong and Mary Jane Lee for a short but enjoyable Hawaiʻi reunion.

Three more Hawaiʻi students entered Yale Law School this semester: Arthur Mori, Raymond Ho and Gary Fujiwara. The Moris' first child, Larry, was born on October 30 and I bought a wool shawl with hood for his baby present. A week later I spent a two-day weekend with Art and Kats and met a lot of Hawaiʻi students who were studying in New York. I spent Christmas 1948 with Art and Kats and met a lot more Hawaiʻi people.

I also got the good news that brother Jimmy might finally be able to come home to Hawaiʻi with his wife Hajime and daughter Keiko.

In my second year, I began to think seriously about how my studies at Yale might or might not fit with Hawaiʻi. I sent twenty-five dollars to have attorney James Morita purchase and send me a copy of the *Revised Laws of Hawaii*. I asked the noted Hawaiʻi attorney Masaji Marumoto to advise me on what subjects to take for my elective courses and, conversely, what subjects would not be so useful when

I returned home.

Most of my second-year classes were "bread and butter law." I was generally more relaxed than in my first year, but the new year studies became more intense as I prepared to take the third semester exams. Law school elections were held, and I was one of four second-year students elected to the executive board. I came in second out of seventeen candidates, due to my being acceptable to both the WASP and Jewish segments of my class. The board in turn elected me treasurer. Bill Shank was our lifelong secretary because of his high popularity, but he always told others I was the most popular guy in the Class of '50.

For the spring term my courses were Property, Corporations, Administrative Law, Evidence and Equity, once more all bread and butter subjects. I also had to present my first mock jury trial.

The news from home was that all my buddies Herbie, Blubber, Unkei, Shikuma and even George Yamamoto were planning on getting married, leaving only Kats and me as the surviving bachelors, without prospects. My April 22 letter home revealed that as against a monthly average "income" of $135, my monthly expenditures (food, rent, books, laundry, postage, recreation, insurance, etc.) averaged $149. It is proof of my perpetual deficit livelihood.

Hawai'i was suffering from a long dock strike in 1949. I felt bad that Dad's business was suffering while he continued to supplement my underfunded GI Bill existence. I have to be eternally grateful to Dad, who sacrificed a lot to keep me afloat. I realized that I could not return home for summer vacation, so I had to start making summer job inquiries from around March, but I was finding summer jobs to be scarce everywhere. My inquiries were negative, increasing my concern over how I was to spend the summer. Two federal officials with strong ties to Hawai'i, Arnold Wills of the National Labor Relations Board and Robert Shivers of the FBI, inquired into summer work in Washington, D.C., but no jobs turned up. So during Easter vacation I went down to D.C. to look around myself. After an interview with the big law firm of Arnold, Fortas & Porter, which was somewhere on 16th Street NW, I remembered this was the street that a wartime friend, Ann Kurimoto, lived on.

When I knocked on the door, a lovely young lady answered. Her name was Fuku Yokoyama. Unbeknown to me at the moment, she was destined to become my lifelong love and mate.

It could have been on this trip that I managed to get a clerkship job for the summer with Joe Farrington, the Territory of Hawaiʻi's (nonvoting) delegate to the US House of Representatives. Through whom and how I got this job I cannot recall, but I suspect that the perennial fixer-upper Hung Wai Ching may have had something to do with it, since he was close to Joe Farrington. At any rate I could not have asked for a better job than being a legislative clerk for the delegate from Hawaiʻi, because the work correlated nicely with my law studies. Learning about legislation affecting the problems of Hawaiʻi, researching Hawaiian law, the tracing of bills through the legislative process, preparation for committee hearings, attendance at hearings, the writing of memorandums in support of legislation and the general knowledge gained on the legislative process, these were enriching.

Mr. Farrington was a warm and caring person who took pains to make my work a great educational experience for me. He was a Republican, and while Hawaiʻi was soon to go Democratic I gained a lot of admiration and respect for him and felt he served Hawaiʻi well. I particularly remember him taking me to call on Mike Masaoka of the Japanese American Citizens League several times to gain his support of statehood for Hawaiʻi. Masaoka gave us a cold reception each time, so I lost all respect for the man.

Otherwise I remember the terrible heat and humidity of the Capitol during summer, which discouraged any outside activity after work hours. I had little social life, since I had no friends there. I can recall seeing Fuku only twice in that early phase of our getting acquainted. Could I have been that busy working at Farrington's office? No answers!

Harry Tanaka and Frank Loo were the new students from Hawaiʻi entering Yale Law School. Having already survived the first two years, my third and last year at law school promised to be more pleasant. My letters show that I went up to spend the weekend in Boston for the Yale-Harvard game, joined by nine couples of Hawaiʻi students who were schooling in that area. In December the law school sponsored a public affairs conference featuring a lot of famous names. Henry Wallace, Thurmond Arnold, Bernard DeVoto and Morris Ernst shared new and radical ideas that one would never hear in Hawaiʻi, and to participate was an advantage only a big school such as Yale could offer.

I again concentrated on courses with practical application to future law practice, minimizing the policy and theory side. We were counseled to take anything that a big-name professor would teach, and in this regard I must specifically mention studying labor law under Professor Harry Schulman. In the late 1940s, Harry Schulman was one of the leading arbitrators in the country. He was a permanent umpire between Ford Motor and the United Auto Workers and was referred to as "the Solomon of the auto industry." Years later people would regard me with awe when they found out I learned my labor law from Harry Schulman. Little did I realize what a significant impact that his class would have on my future practice.

Otherwise my final year in law school was unremarkable. Studies went smoothly, and I was able to start job hunting. I had time to participate in student government as treasurer of the executive board. I was also active in the Barrister's Union, while scholastically I finished in the upper one third of the class. In retrospect, getting my legal education and training at Yale Law School turned out to be among the most fulfilling, enriching and pleasant three years of my life.

I had started to correspond with Fuku and invited her to attend one of the football weekends. She met Art and Sachi Mori and became acquainted with my classmates, Bill Shank, Jerry Katcher, Jerry Preston, Charlie Parker, Andy Wood and others. Our courtship flourished and culminated in her attending my graduation from law school in June of 1950.

Marriage and Family

My chance acquaintance with Fuku was rooted in that moment in August 1943, when I stopped over in Washington, D.C. on our unit's last furlough, a few days before we were to ship out overseas.

I called on Kazuo Yamane, who was on MIS assignment at the Pentagon to see if we could get together. He asked if my army buddy Ruffie Nakahara and I would like to go out on dates with girls. We female-starved GIs said, "Sure!" I never forgot Kazuo's next question: "What kine date you like, haole or Japanee?" to which we grandly responded, "Any kine!" Later Kazuo called to announce that the haole girls were busy that night but his fiancée Mary Shioyama would bring her two Nisei girlfriends and that we would go to the La Madrillion restaurant for dinner.

My buddy Ruffie Nakahara was paired with Ann Kurimoto and I was paired with a young lady named Ida Murata. Both were from the Seattle area. They were quite attractive and formally dressed, wearing little hats with tiny veils across their eyes. They smoked cigarettes with long cigarette holders and drank Scotch on the rocks. This was pretty big-time classy stuff for these two yokels from Hawai'i!

Ann Kurimoto had a warm and outgoing personality, and she kept in touch with both of us throughout the war with Christmas cards and letters. I heard that my date, Ida, met another MIS on a pass and got married to him within a month. Close call! Five years passed before I went to Ann's door in Washington, D.C. and, it was then that I met Fuku, Ann's roommate. She invited me in while she called Ann at work to tell her that she had a visitor, and then she entertained me with conversation until Ann got home.

Fuku Yokoyama was born on October 20, 1924, in Salinas, California. She was the first of five children of Tsugio and Fusae Yokoyama. Her father's background was in the northern island of Hokkaido and the Aizu Wakamatsu area of northern Honshu (the main island). Tsugio Yokoyama was a well-educated man. He had attended Tokyo University and the University of California, and he was genuinely bilingual. He immigrated to California around 1912 and settled in the Salinas area, engaging in large-scale vegetable farming. He was recognized as a leader in the Japanese community in the Salinas Valley, and many people came to seek his counsel. He wrote for the *Shin Sekai* newspaper in San Francisco. He also was a renowned martial arts (kendo) instructor.

The Yokoyama family enjoyed a comfortable middle-class existence. They owned their own home and were able to afford amenities, such as music lessons, for the children. Fuku was a good student, always at the top of her class in the Salinas public schools. Friends told me she would frequently help her classmates with their homework. The Yokoyama children were educated at both English and Japanese language schools and were steeped in the cultural customs and mores of Japan, far more so than most of us in Hawai'i. Fuku could sing patriotic songs of prewar Japan that I had never heard.

Japan's attack on December 7, 1941, brought their world crashing down. Fuku felt angry against Japan for this outrage and for the suffering it inflicted on the innocent people of Japanese ancestry in America. Within a few weeks the FBI came to the Yokoyama home in Salinas and turned the house upside down, including the sacred Butsudan altar, looking for seditious materials. They took away Fuku's father, who she was not to see again for several years. Fuku was just sixteen years old and in high school at the time, but she had to become the head of the household for her mother, an alien illiterate in English, and her four younger brothers and sisters. Without her father, the family farming operations came to a standstill.

In February 1942 President Roosevelt signed Executive Order 9066, which authorized the military commander of the Western Defense Command (California, Oregon and Washington) to remove all persons of Japanese ancestry to "relocation camps" scattered over wastelands of the interior states. The commander in question was the same General DeWitt who Hung Wai Ching had confronted at the Presidio in San Francisco. In April 1942, the Yokoyama family along with all other persons of Japanese ancestry were ordered with only forty-eight hours' notice to leave their homes and take only what they could carry to an assembly center, the Salinas Rodeo grounds. The Yokoyamas lost their home, farming business and all their possessions. These were worth tens of thousands of dollars. They had only their clothing and what few belongings they could carry with them.

Along with 110,000 other persons of Japanese ancestry, the Yokoyamas became victims of the infamous mass evacuation and internment of World War II, the greatest violation of constitutional rights in American history, solely because their names and faces resembled those of Japan. As young as she was, Fuku did not go meekly, with head bowed. When the principal at Salinas High School called all Nisei students to a special assembly, she stood up and said, "We are all loyal American citizens. We want you and the other students of this school to know that. This is the only country that we know. We are not the enemy, and neither are our parents. Please know that no matter what happens, we are Americans, just like you."

Minus her father, the Yokoyamas were put on a train and taken to the Poston Evacuation Center, along the California-Arizona border in the wild, broiling hot desert where the temperature could reach one hundred and twenty degrees in the shade. Fuku hardly ever spoke in any detail about life in the Poston concentration camp, much less write a comprehensive story about that whole tragic experience, probably because it was too painful a memory. I hoped she would do so, for the sake of her children, grandchildren and the generations to follow, and for the sake of history as well. We get little glimpses of her life behind the barbed wire fences through light stories and anecdotes she submitted to *The Hawai'i Herald* for its holiday issues, like "Corporal Sam's Cookies," "The Dust Storm," "The Remembering Tree" and others, but that whole experience as prisoners of their own government and its impact upon their lives, as unjustly bitter and tragic as it was, should be told in detail in our family history.

As a student at Poston High School, Fuku got a job as a reporter for the camp newspaper, *The Poston Chronicle*, where she honed her already developing skills in writing. She devoted herself to making the best of a miserable and horrible existence, which was euphemistically called the Poston War Relocation Camp.

One night in early 1944 the family's barracks room door opened and their father walked in. His hair was all white and his face was creased from age and hardship. With typical Japanese stoicism of gaman and *shikataganai*, he never told his children of his bitter experiences in the Department of Justice camps at Lordsburg and Santa Fe, New Mexico. But at least the Yokoyamas were now all reunited as family once again.

Her parents decided it was time for Fuku to continue her education outside, so she got a scholarship to study nursing at Episcopal Hospital in Philadelphia. After four years of study and training, she received her nursing degree. She passed the Pennsylvania State Boards in 1948 and got her first job as a nurse at Georgetown University Hospital in Washington, D.C.

So it was fortuitous destiny that our paths would cross that early spring day in Washington, D.C. According to her account of our first encounter, she was minding her own business at home "when this guy comes knocking on the door looking for Ann." I was interested in seeing her again when I went to work that summer of 1949 in Washington, D.C. Although I can only remember two occasions that I saw Fuku, once at a JACL picnic and another time when I drove her to Hains Point park to play tennis, Fuku says we met more times than that.

She accepted my invitations to come up for visits to Yale, so I guess I was making a little headway. Being a better writer than talker, it must have been my letters that made my case and carried the day with her, notwithstanding our geographical separation. She has not forgotten some of my epistolary overtures and says she even kept some of my letters, like one in which I wrote that I would check my mailbox daily for any word from her, sticking my hand in the mailbox and only drawing cobwebs! (Translation: "I live for only one kind letter from you!")

My family back home had no inkling that I had developed an interest in this engaging young lady from the Mainland while I was supposed to be seriously studying to become a lawyer. By the time I had taken my final exams in May of 1950, I must have made up my mind that this was the woman I wanted to be my mate for life, and apparently by then the feeling was mutual. It was in this spirit that I invited her to New Haven for my graduation.

She always remembered befriending an awed but proud Jewish

couple who came to the graduation of their son, Irving Morris, and to this day Irving has never forgotten Fuku's kindness to his parents that day. By then Fuku was well known to many of my classmates.

After graduation, I went down to Washington, D.C. to spend more time with Fuku. One evening in June we strolled through the mall and across the Potomac River to the Lincoln Memorial. I proposed to Fuku on the steps of the memorial. To my great joy and relief, she accepted. So those steps halfway up on the right-hand side of the Lincoln Memorial have become hallowed ground ever since for both of us! After that Fuku took a few days off work so we could visit her family.

Her family was living at Bridgeton, New Jersey, at a place called Seabrook Farms. At war's end, they had nothing to return to in California. Along with hundreds of other desperate families, they went from the concentration camp to Seabrook Farms. Seabrook was a frozen food business that paid subpar wages to Japanese who were, the business realized, disciplined and diligent workers. One afternoon at Seabrook, I took a walk with her father. Without any support or intercession of a traditional *baishakunin* (go-between), I asked him for her daughter's hand. I will remember to my dying day he never said yes, but neither did he say no. I parted his company concluding that he had actually approved. Fuku assured me that he admired and appreciated my being direct and gutsy enough to ask for his approval without any go-between to plead my case. Sumio Okabayashi, who later courted and married Fuku's younger sister Hisako, had the same experience. He got a noncommittal response when he went to see Father Yokoyama to ask for Hisako's hand, and we always have a good laugh about that.

Never was I ever to doubt that I had made the right decision. Fuku was a beautiful young lady with a warm and radiant personality. She easily communicated with and related to other people. She got along with everyone, from the mighty to the lowliest. With all she had going for her, she was down to earth and never conceited. She was well accepted and popular with her peers. She had a very bright mind and intellect, with a constant yearning to learn more, and she could carry on a good conversation on almost any subject. She was self-assured and made everyone else comfortable. Everyone was favorably impressed. She was head and shoulders above any girl I had ever known.

Coincidentally, Fuku was chosen in 1949 to represent Washington, D.C. in the Japanese American Citizens League Miss Nisei contest at the JACL Convention in Chicago. She was elected JACL Miss Nisei of 1950 over contestants from JACL chapters all over the country. Her fame and honor reached all the way to Hawai'i, where Judge Sam King always addressed Fuku as "Miss Nisei." Wow, this meant that I was going to be married to the top Nisei girl in America!

I vowed I would not ask her to Hawai'i until I passed the bar examination and got a job with which I could adequately support her as my wife. I returned to Hawai'i that summer and immersed myself in studying for the bar examination, which I approached with serious determination and no fooling around. Preparation was difficult because all legal subjects were specific "black letter" law, whereas my legal education at Yale Law School was more broadly theoretical despite my attempts to keep the coursework close to legal basics. My background was determined by the fact that Yale tended to focus on the philosophy of law, in contrast to a traditional school like Harvard, where law was taught like the Ten Commandments chiseled into stone tablets.

The tension and anxiety of preparing for the bar exam tied my stomach into knots. We took the exam in October 1950. The Board of Bar Examiners was a tough but distinguished group that included top lawyers and several future jurists, such as Bernard Levinson, Russell Cades, Sam King, Sam Landau and Betty Vitousek. On December 15, 1950, I found my name on a list of those who had passed! The supreme court order said that only fifteen of forty-five applicants passed. I was later told they actually passed five of us on the first round. How my fellow attorney Vincent Yano (later a state senator) found out, I don't know, but he used to go around telling people that I had the second highest exam score. Whatever the score, I was assured that I would now become a lawyer. The great weight was lifted from my shoulders.

The first to be told was Fuku. She quit her job at Georgetown Hospital and prepared to move to Hawai'i. I was now able to buy my first car, a Chevrolet sedan, which she picked up on the East Coast. She loaded her possessions in the car, and she and her brother Taro drove all the way to the West Coast via the southern route, stopping on the way to visit their brother Ryuji, who was in basic training at Fort McClellan, Alabama. Fuku boarded the *Lurline* and arrived in late January 1951. She stayed at Ben and Daisy Takayesu's home until the wedding. Daisy was a schoolmate with Fuku at Episcopal Hospital Nursing School in Philadelphia in the late 1940s and had become a "big sister" who helped plan the wedding.

The date was set for February 17. Fuku asked her best friend from nursing school days, Jackie Drew, to come to Hawai'i to be her maid of honor. The popular dentist Dr. Katsumi Kometani, who had gone off to war as the morale officer of the 100th Battalion, walked Fuku down the aisle. My brother Jimmy, back from Japan, was my best man. Various friends and family served as bridesmaids and groomsmen, including my good pals from the VVV and 442. True to the traditions set by my parents, we were married in the Harris Memorial Church, with the Reverend Harry Komuro leading us in making our vows.

As a sign of the changing times, the wedding was covered in detail by *The Honolulu Advertiser*. Of the two daily newspapers, the *Advertiser* up to and during the war had ridden the banner of the "Yellow Peril" while puffing up the doings of the Big Five and the descendants of privilege. Now the newspaper described our altar flowers and the flowers in the corsages. It reported that Fuku wore a white brocade gown that was designed in her home city, which the newspaper identified as Washington, D.C. It did say that she was formerly of Salinas, California, but there was no hint of what she or her family had been put through, other than, possibly, that her parents were unable to attend.

My only concern for the atmosphere around our wedding was the cultural distance between Hawai'i Japanese and Fuku, who was not only from the Mainland but the JACL's Miss Nisei. One of the women who attended the wedding actually said, "I don't like kotonks…the only one I like is Fuku!" Suffice it to say, Fuku charmed everyone.

After the wedding, we had a reception across the street at the Nuʻuanu YMCA. The location had a certain symmetry to it, in that Nuʻuanu YMCA was where Hung Wai Ching had performed such great work as director of youth programs, and where the Morale Section and the Emergency Service Committee had headquartered during the war. The *Advertiser* reported that instead of a nine-course Chinese dinner, we had punch and cookies. Several people told us, "You are so brave to just have a simple reception." The truth was we were not brave but broke. We weren't going deeply into debt to provide a lavish feast for the wedding guests, which was the custom of the time, and we may have pioneered a trend for a more sensible wedding reception for other young newlyweds to follow. 🌺

Part Four

A Lawyer's Life

Family Man

While in the military, I spent a great deal of time thinking about the future of Hawaiʻi, as I indicated. I wanted a changed Hawaiʻi based on the idea of equality, a Hawaiʻi of opportunity in which individuals could rise according to their ability and hard work. I was far from alone. Many people, particularly many veterans, engaged in discussions along this line.

As we prepared to depart the West Coast for the India-Burma theater, I had written my long letter that had become an essay entitled "Our New Hawaii." It seemed testamentary in mood, written by a soldier who might not possibly return home. It conveyed my yearning for a Hawaiʻi that many of us were willing to fight for.

I wondered if I was being too idealistic, but I believed the idea of a new Hawaiʻi reflected "the gleanings of talks I had had with the boys and the inner thoughts of their letters."

I can't read this essay today without blushing at such flamboyant rhetoric and visionary daydreaming. But while I no longer entertain such soaring thoughts, or at least such soaring rhetoric, I feel I reflected the mindset of the Nisei youth who went off to war. We were committed to struggling for our generation and for future generations. When the war was over, many pursued this dream of a new Hawaiʻi by direct involvement in politics or the labor movement. I took a somewhat different path.

I had a law degree from a prestigious university, but it guaranteed nothing. I needed to establish myself in the legal profession. Fuku was a trained nurse. We two, along with many others, had to make our way through numerous everyday issues while somehow finding expression for our lofty goals.

The story of our married and family life could take a book of its own. Our first home was a duplex apartment on Ala Wai Boulevard that I rented several weeks in advance of Fuku's arrival. It was not in such good shape, so Roy Nakada helped me paint the interior to make it fit for my new bride. In appreciation, Roy was our first guest after we settled in. Fuku served him waffles from a waffle iron that was one of our wedding gifts, but the waffles stuck to the iron. It was not sufficiently larded with oil, and Roy never let Fuku forget her first breakfast offering.

Then there was an old blonde woman who lived in the other duplex. She used to pound on the wall to make us tone down our radio or shout out other complaints, so I quickly started to look for another place, notwithstanding the work we had just put into our newly painted apartment.

Hung Wai's wife, Elsie Ching, saved the day. She asked Fuku if we would be interested in a nearby cottage owned by her sister. Fuku checked it out and accepted on the spot. It was one of eight or nine cottages with an open grassy courtyard at the end of Tusitala Street, off Kaiulani Avenue in what then was a residential section of Waikīkī. The cottages were home to racially mixed families with kids. There were old wooden, termite-eaten structures with ancient plumbing, but the rent was reasonable and we didn't have to share the cottage with a cranky lady, so we moved right in. We have pleasant memories of our first three or four years living in the Tusitala Street cottage.

Our daughter Sandy was born while we lived there, and this was also home to the first of our many Boxer dogs. Rusty was given to us by Kazuo Yamane, and I well remember bringing Rusty home covered with dried dog poop and giving him his first bath in the outdoor laundry sink in the back of the cottage. Fuku would wheel Sandy in a stroller with Rusty on a leash out to Kalākaua Avenue. She tied Rusty to a gum machine at the entrance before going into the drugstore to shop, only to find Rusty following her into the store dragging the gum machine behind him. I can still visualize Rusty sprawled out on the living room floor while Sandy crawled over him, pulling his ears while he lay in blissful contentment. Sandy has never stopped loving Boxer dogs ever since.

We were by no measure well-off but we were not impoverished either. While I waited for the bar exam results, I briefly was associated with Norman Chung, a brilliant attorney who I had known from Aliiolani Elementary School, when I was classmate of his sister Mary. After I passed the bar, I came face to face with the fact that the Hawai'i legal profession was still largely segregated. A young Nisei lawyer could only expect to be hired by a local lawyer or local law firm, since the haole Big Five law firms still did not hire Nisei or other locals, probably because their big business clients would not want to be serviced or advised by locals. In this and many other ways, the goals for which we had fought in the war were far from being realized.

Soon after Fuku's arrival in Hawai'i, she learned firsthand of the employment glass ceiling faced by local Japanese. She took her visiting maid of honor, Jackie Drew, with her to a job interview at Queen's Hospital. The haole personnel director offered Jackie a job on the spot while hardly considering Fuku, who was the only job seeker for the interview.

Fuku next got a line on a nursing job at Straub Medical Clinic through the ever-helpful Daisy Takayesu. Straub did not hire Japanese doctors but nurses were another case. Daisy worked for Straub and her recommendation of Fuku was quickly accepted by the clinic. Fuku was fortunate to be assigned to Dr. Herbert Bowles, who came from a family of Christian missionaries to Japan. Dr. Bowles was partial to Japanese and even took the trouble to learn Japanese medical terms to better treat his elderly Issei patients. Working at Straub was a good learning ground for Fuku to become oriented and adjusted to the ways of Hawai'i. When Fuku conversed freely with Dr. Bowles and even joked with him, the old-time nurse aides used to marvel: "Chee, you no scared talk to da haoles, yeh?" To which Fuku replied,

"Why not, they're just like anybody else." Once when Fuku admitted other local patients from the waiting room ahead of an old haole dowager, an aide admonished Fuku by saying, "You supposed to let her in first, she's Big Five wife," to which Fuku responded, "Why shouldn't she wait, the others came ahead of her." Then she asked Dr. Bowles, "What's the Big Five?" to his great amusement. Quite often, locals would ask Fuku, "You from da Mainland, yeh?" Over all the years Fuku never learned to talk authentic pidgin, so our kids used to tell her not to try, "because it just don't sound right."

Job discrimination in the hospitals was far from the only remainder of the prewar order that continued as we started our married life. The Elks Club, the Pacific Club and the Waialae Golf Club still barred Asians from membership and, as I indicated, my own employment options were confined to Japanese-American firms. Thankfully, these firms were the gold standard of law practice.

I received one offer from Tsukiyama & Yamaguchi and a second offer from Masaji Marumoto. Wilfred Tsukiyama was the second most senior Nisei lawyer in Hawai'i. He was a prominent public figure who was idolized by the local Japanese community for his eloquent oratory and political success. He had served as Honolulu City and County attorney and territorial senator and was on his way to becoming chief justice of the Hawai'i Supreme Court. It would have been a feather in my cap to work for his law firm. With a name like "Tsukiyama" many people assumed even without asking that I was his son, but as I often have said, I would not trade my father Seinosuke Tsukiyama for any other person in the world, no matter how famous.

Masaji Marumoto kept a lower profile but was much respected for his brilliant legal mind. He had just broken up his long partnership with the distinguished Robert Murakami and was in need of a legal associate to help him in his practice. He was also a close family friend. For me, there was no choice but to work for Masaji Marumoto. I associated with him at a starting salary of $200 per month.

Masaji Marumoto was a genius, or at least a near-genius. He was a graduate of Harvard Law School and eventually was appointed not once but twice to the Supreme Court, first by a Republican governor and then by a Democrat. He had an amazing power of focus and concentration. He could be walking down the street deep in a legal problem. If a passing friend greeted him, Marumoto might not see or hear him. I early learned to leave him alone until late in the afternoon after he had completed the day's assignments and had emerged from his spell of intense concentration. His demeanor would be best described as *majime na* (serious) and conscientious and not given to developing warm human relationships. He was a tough and demanding boss who expected only the best out of you. So my first law job promised to be a good learning and training environment, but it didn't work out that way. His practice consisted of mostly complex business and tax problems that were over my head. Furthermore, Marumoto was so well versed in practically everything he encountered that he didn't need much research assistance. He also had a hard time delegating even the simplest work because the clients wouldn't let him. He once gave me an uncontested divorce to handle but the client protested and wanted "the old man himself."

I began to realize that what Maru really needed was an experienced partner rather than a fledging associate. As the year went by, the attorney Suyeki Okumura notified me of a vacancy at the City and County Attorney's Office at a much better salary, and I decided to accept. I made an amicable agreement with Marumoto to leave his law firm for public law work at the city.

However brief the relationship, I benefited. He had a great work ethic and good client relationships. He stressed the importance of an attorney maintaining an independent arm's length from his clients, never partnering with or investing in a client's project or business. That was why Marumoto never got rich, and neither did I in my almost sixty years of law practice thereafter.

I became a deputy City and County attorney under James Morita. This was during the administration of the legendary Mayor John H. Wilson, who was then well into his eighties and showing his age. City government was run by his "kitchen cabinet" of Herbert Kum and Takaichi Miyamoto, two old-timer Democrat politicians who dispensed political patronage on Wilson's behalf. I had to sign a Democratic Party card to get the job, and that is how I became a Democrat by political faith. The City and County Attorney's Office was staffed with nine attorneys at the time including Okumura, Frank McKinley, Moon Chan, Vernon Tashima, Dan Moon, Frank Rothwell and Hiroshi Sakai. In addition to providing counsel to the departments and writing opinions, we were assigned to litigating in court.

The court work started with paternity prosecutions and condemnation cases, both involving jury trials, so we got good trial experience. One case involved a charming city bus driver who looked like Clark Gable. He was apparently irresistible to female passengers on his Kalihi line. I had to file three separate paternity actions against him. I asked him, "Eh, dis da t'ird time already. How come you no can keep your pants on?" to which he replied, "Eh, if da *wahin*e lie down and spread her legs, you goin' only stand ova deah and look!"

One unforgettable assignment was the Izumo Taisha case in which a Shinto sect sued the city to recover its temple in Palama, claiming the city had taken it over during the war under duress. The Board of Supervisors was sympathetic to Izumo Taisha's claim, eager as they were to cultivate the so-called "Japanese vote," which was about forty percent of the electorate at that time. Defending against this claim would thus become a *shibai* and politically an unpopular cause. Frank McKinley was assigned to this case. He combed the city attorney's staff for assistance, but all of the old-timers were smart enough to duck out, leaving only me at the bottom of the totem pole. It was a highly publicized case with overflowing crowds and daily photos in the newspapers, making it a most embarrassing and uncomfortable experience for a Nisei.

Around this time, as young and inexperienced as I was and for reasons unknown to me, I was appointed by the Supreme Court to the territorial Board of Bar Examiners. I was assigned to administer the questions on contracts. After every October bar exam, the examiners would be sequestered on a Friday in one of the Waikīkī hotels to grade the examinees' answers in our respective fields of law. We couldn't get out until we finished grading, which usually took until Sunday. My roommate was the attorney Ray Torkildson, who would always show up with a bottle of Jim Beam sour mash whiskey. With my help, it would be emptied by the time we got out. I served as a bar examiner for well over twenty years because Chief Justice William S. Richardson would not accept my resignation, no matter that I eventually became the longest-serving examiner on the board.

As a resident of City Hall, the 1954 mayoralty election was unforgettable. A young upstart, Frank F. Fasi, dared to run against the venerable "Johnny" Wilson in the primary. Ordinarily Fasi would have been smashed. But the Republican Party people jumped into the Democratic primary race and voted for Fasi, causing Wilson's defeat. In the general election, they voted their fellow Republican Neal S. Blaisdell into the mayor's office. Loyal Democrats never forgot nor forgave Frank Fasi for his treachery, myself included.

The Board of Supervisors (later called the City Council), comprised of five Democrats out of seven board seats, was determined to maintain—as "holdovers"—the Democratically appointed City and County attorney Morita (as well as building superintendent Arthur Akinaka and city physician Dr. Thomas Mossman) by refusing to confirm incoming Mayor Blaisdell's appointments. The territorial government through its Attorney General Edward Sylva filed a quo warranto action in the supreme court challenging Morita's de facto title as holdover. The city Board of Supervisors hired two distinguished attorneys, Michio Watanabe and Yasutaka Fukushima, to defend Morita, and assigned the two youngest staff attorneys to do the research. I was one. I spent two whole nights in the supreme court library looking for cases upholding Morita's holdover status. All were in our favor except for an ancient Missouri case. Then the unthinkable happened when the two Democratic-appointed justices, Edward Towse and Ingram Stainback, split. Stainback joined Republican Phillip Rice to write the majority opinion, relying on that one Missouri case, effectively ending Morita's tenure.

Mayor Blaisdell appointed Norman Chung to be the new City and County attorney. This was the same Norman Chung for whom I briefly had worked before passing the bar. Chung was a strict boss and taskmaster. When he retained me along with a few other Morita appointees, he held an ax over our heads by requiring us to sign undated letters of resignation, which meant he could fire us at any moment. I was put in charge of the Opinion Section, responsible for supervising all written opinions issued by the city attorney. If in Chung's opinion there was a poorly drafted opinion, he would not criticize the writer but would call me in and chew me out, saying, "What do you mean allowing this kind of crap to come over to my desk for signature!" I wrote many opinions myself. When my son Paul worked as a deputy Corporation Counsel many years later, he found various opinions I had written in the 1950s that were still in effect.

Chung was a good courtroom lawyer, and he assigned me to participate in some of the jury trials, from which I learned the importance of jury selection. I well remember serving as his associate counsel in the contested condemnation of the Waikiki Tavern for expansion of the Waikīkī beachfront. The landowner was represented by the great Garner Anthony, an influential corporate lawyer famed for his opposition to martial law during the war. Anthony was charming, eloquent and had movie star looks. During jury selection we noticed one Waialae-Kahala haole woman practically swooning over Anthony's every word and move, presaging one sure vote for his case before the jury. When Norman Chung rejected her on his peremptory challenges, Garner Anthony sidled up and whispered, "Can we talk settlement?"

I learned there is no sure outcome to a jury trial. Going to a jury is like shooting craps. This lesson lay behind my eventual advocacy of alternate dispute resolution (ADR), in all its forms, as an alternative to jury-trial litigation.

Government condemnation of property for public purposes became one of my areas of specialization. For example, I was assigned to appeal the US Navy's condemnation of the city streets in the Pearl Harbor area for $1. This included a city water system worth $88,256. I filed a motion for relief in the Federal Court of Appeals and went to San Francisco to argue the city's case in the 9th Circuit Court of Appeals. The three appeal judges sat there while their clerks took notes. Their ruling, probably written by those law clerks, sustained the lower court judgment of $1. In other words, it was a real travesty of justice. I lost respect for the Federal Courts as a result. It strengthened my conviction that one cannot always expect to get justice in a judicial process that is administered by fallible human beings. All told, I spent five years as a government attorney with the city. I acquired legal knowledge and legal skills related to public governance that I could not have learned in a private law office. These were to serve me in good stead.

In late 1956, Suyeki Okumura contacted me. This was the same person who originally had brought me into the city attorney's office. He then had left for private practice. He asked if I would like to associate myself with him, and I accepted. Suyeki had a great pedigree as the son of the Reverend Takie Okumura, a Christian missionary from Japan who built the Makiki Christian Church, among many other things. He was one of the several most important leaders of Hawai'i's Japanese community in the earlier part of the century. In contrast to his famous father, Suyeki was a low-key, low-profile person. He was a sound lawyer. He did not offer me a partnership deal but an associate fee-splitting relationship, which I accepted.

My Private Practice

I started out with three good sources of work, the Honolulu Redevelopment Agency (HRA), labor-management arbitrations and my friend Kazuo Yamane's family businesses. My counsel as a city attorney to the Redevelopment Agency apparently impressed its manager, Edward Burns, who was the brother of Jack Burns, at that time the new chairman of the revived Democratic Party. Ed Burns gave me a contract that kept me busy and provided a good source of income for at least the next decade. The HRA was the first Hawai'i participant in the federally funded slum clearance program under the HHFA (Housing and Home Finance Agency) and was created as an autonomous public corporation under the City and County of Honolulu with its own governing board. The principal target of the slum clearance program was the "slum" area occupied by minority groups bounded by

A troop ship carrying Nisei soldiers approaches Aloha Tower during homecoming in Honolulu Harbor.

Hawai'i welcomes the 442nd home.

After returning to civilian life, I approached my studies with a new discipline.

Top: Home from the war, I receive a warm send-off to Indiana University (above), where I was the first American of Japanese ancestry enrolled.

Top and above: *In my dorm room and on campus at Yale, where I was the first AJA to enroll in Yale Law School.*

My fiancée Fuku Yokoyama as national Miss Nisei in 1950.

Top: My wife, Fuku, was a great mother and grandmother too. **Above:** Fuku and I with our children Tim, Paul and Sandy.

Top: *With grandson Jordan de Oliveira and a Japanese red pine bonsai, a gift from the Japanese imperial family.* ***Above:*** *Our expanding 'ohana.*

Beretania Street, Liliha Street, Emma Street and the H-1 Freeway. I served as legal advisor to Ed Burns, handled the legal dealings with the HHFA, drafted the negotiated settlement deals and handled the condemnation cases if an owner balked at selling.

The most innovative area of my practice was arbitration. Again, this is a topic about which one could write a book.

The Yamane family business covered everything from property development projects to contracts, wills and trusts. After the death of the family business founder, U. Yamane, his son Kazuo consistently brought me a significant portion of their legal business. They were one among a good many family businesses for which I performed similar services.

Despite all the work, those years turned out to be financially unrewarding. As years passed, my earnings actually decreased because of the unfavorable split rather than increase, as one would have expected.

While income was declining, our costs of living were rising, resulting from the complexity of our lives. All three of our children were born in the ten-year period following our marriage. After Sandy in 1953 came Paul Tsugio, who was born on April 17, 1955, followed by Timothy Ken, who was born on March 31, 1959 (in the year Hawai'i was granted statehood).

We built a second small house on my parents' property on Akaka Place and moved in. It was tight and cozy but it housed the four of us until Timmy came along, when we switched with Grandpa and Grandma and moved to the big house at Akaka. As a result, our children were fortunate enough to intimately know and grow up with Grandpa and Grandma Tsukiyama.

Around 1964, Fuku started to take classes at UH toward an academic college degree that she had never had a chance to pursue. She always aspired to a full education, and to her great credit she earned her degree from UH in the years that followed.

We also put a priority on travel. Fuku's mother met her first two Tsukiyama grandchildren in 1955, when she stopped off in Hawai'i on her way back from Japan. Two years later, Fuku took the two to New Jersey for a visit. In 1961 Grandpa Yokoyama also got to meet

Tim. Grandpa passed away the same year, and we attended his memorial service. Afterward, I bought a Chevrolet station wagon in Philadelphia. We drove the family all the way cross-country, exploring the vastness of the American continent and visiting friends from the war and college years. We made stops in New Haven, New York City, Niagara Falls, Chicago, Minneapolis, South Dakota, Yellowstone Park (the kids' first snow), Spokane, Seattle, Portland and San Francisco. This was the sixth year of Hawai'i's statehood, and there was a strong sense at work about discovering the country. By this time the kids were twelve, ten and six respectively, and they remembered the smallest detail of that trip, which bore out the Japanese adage "*kawai ko ni tabi wo sase*" (for endearing children, send them out to travel).

In the summer of 1969, Fuku took a UH world educational tour, and I sent Sandy in my place. I always say that was some of the best money I ever spent because it took Sandy out of her narrow high school sophomore mode and opened up the whole world as a learning experience. At one point in Europe she remarked, "Look at all these haoles, and none of them speak English!"

Both of the boys were playing baseball and, while Sandy and Mom were gone, I took them for a baseball tour through San Francisco and Los Angeles. We got to see baseball immortals such as Willie Mays, Willie McCovey, Juan Marichal and Sandy Koufax. These years were in the "hippie" era when many of our nation's youth went to pot, but we can thankfully say that our kids never got lost or got into trouble. As for other travel, around 1968 I took the first of a number of trips to Japan, this time on behalf of a client who was attempting to secure a patent from the Japanese government.

At the beginning of 1967 I withdrew from Okumura & Takushi, citing financial hardship. I struck out on my own as a sole practitioner. On February 1, 1967, I sent out an announcement that I would be opening my own law office at 800 Melim Building at 333 Queen Street, Honolulu.

My leap into solo law practice was aided and abetted by my good friend Alvin Shim, who sublet a portion of his Shim Segal & Tam law firm offices to me. Alvin had a deep client base in the labor movement, and many people relied on him for advice. I did no work for his firm but developed my own clientele. A few days after I settled down in my new office, I got a call from Margaret Nishimoto, one of the secretaries at Okumura & Takushi, who asked if I had hired a law secretary. When I answered, "Not yet," she responded, "Would you consider me?" I said, "I would love to have you but I don't want O & T to think I stole you away," to which she said, "Don't worry, I will be leaving on my own." To have Margaret as my secretary would turn out to be one of the most fortuitous and rewarding aspects of the twenty-three ensuing years of law practice. Margaret was competent, efficient and conscientious. She kept good records, ran the office well, treated the clients courteously and was loyal to the end. I came to look upon her more like a partner than an employee. I included her in our retirement system, and in the end her share was over $100,000.

I continued to have work from the Yamane family and other interesting clients—for example, the United Fishing Agency, the Hawaii Methodist Union and the Hawaii Carpenters Pension Trust Fund. Despite spending much of my time on conventional legal work, I was fortunate to become deeply involved in arbitration, an innovative area of the law, for which I became most identified. That was mediation and arbitration or, broadly, alternative dispute resolution. I caught a trend of the times, for which I seemed to be temperamentally suited.

Alternative Dispute Resolution

I have often been asked, "How did you get to be an arbitrator?" My answer invariably is "It took a lot of luck!" It began when I elected to take the course in labor law by Professor Harry Schulman in my last year at Yale Law School. The conventional wisdom of the time was to take a course not for its subject matter but for its professor, and Schulman had a big reputation. His decisions heavily influenced the course of labor arbitration from its earliest years. If I told prominent national arbitrators that I had taken Harry Schulman's labor course, it would immediately elevate me several notches in their esteem.

Nine years later, as a practicing lawyer, I got a call from Edward H. Nakamura, a scholarly labor lawyer who represented the International Longshoreman and Warehouseman's Union (ILWU). As a child, I passed his home daily on my way to Japanese school. He was a fellow volunteer in the VVV in 1942 and then a fellow gunner in the 522nd Field Artillery Battalion training at Camp Shelby. Ed was a devoted advocate for organized labor in the face of the anti-Communist crusade of the McCarthy era. He would eventually say that many people crossed the street to avoid him, but that I would always greet him with aloha.

The ILWU was one of the most important forces in Hawai'i, a leader in challenging the Big Five oligarchy. The ILWU represented the workers of the sugar and pineapple industry and also the waterfront. Ed told me he had an agreement with an influential lawyer for management, Ernest "Bud" Moore, to put my name on the arbitration panel in the ILWU/pineapple industry contract. Years later, researching the records of the 1959 pineapple negotiations, I read that the head of the ILWU, Jack Hall, was unable to agree with the companies on an arbitration panel. They deferred the matter to their respective lawyers, Myer Symonds for the union and Raymond Torkildson for the pineapple industry, and the selection fell into the hands of their respective associates, Eddie Nakamura and Bud Moore. I told Eddie that I had no arbitration experience, but he assured me, "No worry, you'll do all right." So I am deeply indebted to both the ILWU and the pineapple industry for having the courage to accept me as the first Japanese American into the ranks of Hawai'i labor arbitrators. Previously all were haole. As a result, my five-plus decades of arbitration work commenced in February 1959, short on ability and experience but with lots of luck!

The work was launched and then accelerated on the crest of a huge wave created by the 1960 US Supreme Court "Trilogy" cases, as they were called. These decisions limited the judiciary's power to vacate arbitration awards, thereby upholding the supremacy of arbitration. The decades that followed were considered the golden age of arbitration.

Demand for arbitrations arose from the grievance clauses in collective bargaining agreements governing many segments of the economy: not only sugar and pineapple but airlines, hotels, health care and many other businesses and industries. The grievances usually were filed on behalf of workers by their unions, not only the ILWU but the teamsters, machinists, engineers, electrical workers, transport workers, airline pilots, hotel restaurant workers, nurses, the Newspaper Guild and so on.

The scope of collective bargaining expanded into the public sector in the 1960s, first because bargaining was extended to federal employees, followed by bargaining for employees of the state and county governments (thanks to a 1968 amendment of the Hawai'i State Constitution). As a result of public-sector bargaining, demand for arbitration work nearly doubled during this period.

My earlier decisions cited arbitral text and prior decisions at length to authoritatively support and justify my conclusions. The resulting rulings were not just because I said so but because the weight of well-reasoned arbitration decisions said so. I undertook this extensive research not only to authenticate my decisions but also to educate the parties and myself on the issues at hand.

I will never forget my first case involving a five-man System Board of Adjustment, as it is called. On one side was Pan American Airways and on the other was the Transport Workers Union. Each side sent two members from the Mainland to sit on the board in a bitterly contested case. After the evidence was presented, we went into executive session. A heated discussion erupted, and two big haole board members swung away at each other, with me like a damned fool wading in to stop the fight. That case brought a new definition to the role of a neutral.

I always maintained that a party does not need an attorney to present a winning case. A fire captain was given a minor suspension for an unannounced absence from his station when a raging ten-alarm fire broke out at Sand Island. He was also the president of the union and said, "They can't do this to me!" Rejecting the union's lawyer, he insisted on hiring David Shutter, then the biggest trial lawyer in town. The fire department was represented by a man named Ed Yee, who was a career civil servant but not a lawyer. He was pissing in his pants at the prospect of facing the biggest gun in town. But Dave Shutter could not overcome the total lack of merit in the fire captain's case. My dismissal of the fire captain's grievance converted the lay advocate Ed Yee into the "giant killer who beat the great Shutter!"

From repeated experience, I became better educated in "the law of the workplace." Some of my decisions went beyond my research of arbitration text to overturning long-accepted contractual practices and beliefs. One example was the interpretation of what was known as the "seniority/ability" clauses in sugar and pineapple industry contracts, an issue focused by a disputed promotion at Laupahoehoe Plantation on the Big Island. The union liked the clause as a means of honoring seniority as well as ability. I held it should be read as a "relative ability seniority clause," in which management could first make its selection based on the comparative ability of the applicants. The seniority factor was to come into play only if ability of the applicants was equal or nearly so. Thereafter the union inclination to give great weight to seniority was diminished, prompting the ILWU attorney Jimmy King many years later to complain to me, "You sonnovabitch, ever since the Laupahoehoe decision the union has never won a seniority case again!"

I did not predictably support either labor or business. In one agonizing case, an airline pilot who was terminated for an accident caused by pilot fatigue refused to accept the airline's offer to send him through rehabilitation. Reluctantly, I upheld his termination, based on the fact that he could have saved his job by opting for rehab rather than challenging management's discipline.

One of my arbitrations became widely known as the "pineapple juice" case, which began when a high-level travel executive claimed that a flight attendant threw pineapple juice in his face. She was summarily fired because the airline decided that "heads must roll" to save the company's reputation in the travel industry. Fellow travel executives, flight attendants and passengers testified, telling various conflicting stories of the incident. I fell back on the "what is the truth" theme in Kurosawa's famous movie *Rashomon*, relying on the eyewitness testimony of a hippie passenger who just happened to be there and had no stake in the outcome. He described the incident as an innocent, unintentional accident, which led to my restoring the flight attendant to her job.

Throughout my long work in this field, the institutions dedicated to alternative dispute resolution continued to multiply. Following commencement of federal collective bargaining, I was accepted for practice in the Federal Mediation and Conciliation Service and on the National Mediation Board. As a result I started to get calls to arbitrate at the Pearl Harbor Naval Shipyard, Fort Shafter and other federal agencies, such as the Immigration Naturalization Service and the US Customs Service.

Early on in the 1960s the American Arbitration Association contacted me hoping to become active in Hawai'i. This led to opening the first AAA office in a spare room in my law office. I was placed on the AAA labor dispute panel and also its commercial/construction panel, medical malpractice panel and, eventually, its international commercial dispute panel.

In 1964 Governor Burns appointed me to a ten-year term as chairman of the Hawai'i Employment Relations Board, a purely pro bono job. I was never paid a nickel but nevertheless was mentioned in Cooper and Daws book *Land and Power in Hawaii: The Democratic Years* in connection with the idea that Nisei carpetbaggers were getting rich during the Burns administration from lush political patronage jobs.

In 1966 I was accepted into membership of the prestigious National Academy of Arbitrators, the first Asian arbitrator to be so recognized.

In 1982, following the Iniki Hurricane on Kaua'i, I worked with a national dispute resolution institute, Endispute, setting up arbitration forums to resolve damage claims against insurers.

Incrementally, mediation began to influence or displace arbitration. Under the auspices of the Hawai'i Supreme Court, I became the only arbitrator in Hawai'i to advocate and practice a hybrid "med-arb" wherein the disputing parties agree that the neutral party can first engage in mediating the dispute and, failing agreement, may then proceed to decide the dispute through arbitration. I have successfully resolved thirty or so disputes through med-arb. In the process I have become a staunch advocate of employing a widening range of ADR, alternative dispute resolution.

My appointments have taken me to various places across the Mainland and also to Japan, where the Department of Defense Schools and Overseas Teacher's Association were in conflict. The Defense Department appealed five of my decisions supporting teachers to the Federal Labor Relations agency, which reversed my decisions. However, on appeal, my decisions were reaffirmed by the Federal Circuit Court of Appeals. This court ruling preserved my perfect record of never having any of my arbitration decisions vacated or set aside.

Along the way, I encountered a wide range of stylistic approaches to the arbitration table. The corporate lawyer Bud Moore was one of the best. He knew instinctively that arbitration called for a kind of advocacy that was different from court litigation. He made his points in a calm, low-keyed manner completely devoid of adversarial stridency. He could go through an entire hearing without making a single objection. He would just look at me with a knowing smile when an opposing lawyer asked some outrageous question. He would artfully sum up his whole case in the final oral argument while noting and dismissing the flaws that had emerged in his opponent's case.

In contrast, Laurence "Larry" Silberman was the first of several "pit bulls" who practiced at my arbitration table. He fought for every inch and point for his case. Once he demanded that a hearing be stopped so he could go back to the office to get the authority to show that my ruling was all wet. Most memorably, he faced the great labor leader Jack Hall in a Hawaiʻi Newspaper Agency/Newspaper Guild arbitration. As Silberman goaded and insulted Jack Hall, Hall flushed with anger, so I called a recess. As I walked out, I could hear the newspaper executives telling Silberman to take it easy, to which Silberman's retorted, "Look, you guys be the good guys, and I'll be the prick!" Silberman went on to become the darling of Republican presidents, receiving appointments as an ambassador and then a federal judge.

Several local lawyers were likewise exceptionally aggressive, such as Ben Sigal, Kenneth Nam and Charles Khiem. Not far behind them were Herb Takahashi and Danny Vasconcellos, who converted arbitrations into a Perry Mason courtroom scene. I have consistently maintained that if there is anything wrong with arbitration it is the legal formalities and technicalities such lawyers bring to the process. Arbitration is not and should not be litigation!

From the tension between advocacy and fact-finding arises the question, "Whither arbitration?" The original voice of industrial relations was Professor George Taylor of the Wharton School of Business at the University of Pennsylvania. He saw arbitration as "a substitute for the strike over unresolved grievances" and as an extension of the collective bargaining process. The Taylor approach to arbitration emphasizes problem-solving and minimizing formalities and technicalities. In contrast, the president of the AAA, J. Noble Braden, saw arbitration as a substitute for litigation. In his view, arbitration was a quasi-judicial process, meaning a more court-like process,

Clearly I am of the old school. How I survived so long mystifies me, because to my disappointment the Braden approach seems to be displacing the Taylor model. The influence of lawyers creates a more technical and adversarial environment. It pressures arbitrators to function more and more like judges. As a result, some arbitration commentators predict that eventually labor arbitration will become another branch or segment of the law.

I stubbornly contend that arbitration is an inevitable part and extension of the employer/union collective bargaining process as the parties intended it to be. The underlying problem-solving objective of collective bargaining continues to demand not only that arbitration supplant the strike as an industrial weapon but to avoid, and not emulate, judicial litigation as the means to preserve industrial peace. To be effective, grievance arbitration must basically remain the parties' in-house resolution process, with a high value placed on informality and cost effectiveness. I believe the arbitrator must insist that the lawyers desist from transforming arbitration into a courtroom. The objective is to resolve workplace disputes. Toward this end, I have not hesitated to stop midway in the hearing to urge advocates to negotiate a settlement in situations neither side was likely to win. I also have offered the hybrid approach of med-arb.

Over a more than fifty-year career in arbitration, I was to receive more than a thousand requests to serve as arbitrator. I issued more than eight hundred final written arbitration decisions and awards. Over fifty of those decisions were published in national labor arbitration reports, adding to the body of reasoning and precedent that shapes the field. For young lawyers looking for challenging and gratifying work, I recommend it.

The Art of Bonsai

Going on my arbitration cases to the outside islands starting in late 1960s, I used to inquire who was the "*bonsai* man" in town. I would visit them before I caught the plane back to Honolulu. Most of the individuals I found practiced in lonely isolation, and they were delighted when a stranger would show up and "talk story" in Japanese about their bonsai. They were the living embodiment of the way bonsai somehow had survived the cultural denigration of all things Japanese during World War II.

When I would admire their trees and they would hear me say, "*Kore wa sugoi chokkan da* (This is a superb chokkan.)," or "*Omoshiroi bunjin da ne* (Isn't this an interesting bunjin?)," or "*Kono nishiki wa rippa ni dette masu ne* (This nishiki has developed splendidly.)," they must have thought, *Hey this young kid knows his bonsai!* We became kindred bonsai souls. By the time I was ready to leave, invariably they would reach up on the shelf and hand me a bonsai as *omiyage* (a culturally sensitive gift) and would absolutely refuse to take any money.

They would willingly share their secrets. When I asked a great bonsai man, Bunjiro Okada of the Big Island, what made his plants so green and healthy, he sidled up close to me, pointed to the persimmon tree and whispered that the ashes from the burnt persimmon leaves made "numba one *koyashi*." On Kauaʻi, Sugahara-san took me to meet "Old Man" Honda of Makaweli, whose son Squash Honda was a luna (overseer) at Gay & Robinson Plantation. Squash gained us easy entry into the forbidden pasture land above the cane fields of the plantation, where I dug some of the finest nature-shaped ironwood I have ever seen. It had been pruned by cows munching on the needles. During breaks in the digging, the three of us, Honda, Sugahara and I would sit under a tree and talk story about bonsai from the old days. I still have handwritten copies of the letters of *orei* written in my poor Japanese that I sent to these old-timers, thanking them for their courtesy and bonsai friendship.

I had become a bonsai "nut." I had joined a network of bonsai practitioners that then were all but unknown. If my family and the subject of history were, together, my deepest passions, bonsai was next, a kind of parallel project of intense interest in nature. It was an exploration that connected me with plants, ideas and growers that I found incomparably interesting.

For me bonsai started in 1964 when I responded to a Department of Education notice of an adult education bonsai class at Ka'imukī High School. I showed up every Thursday night after playing golf and having a few beers with the old farts at the Ala Wai Golf Course, sleeping off the beers for the first hour and then muddling through a mediocre, disorganized class. The instructor used to display his bonsai planted in old cooking pots or rusted enamel tubs, which should give you an idea of the quality of my bonsai education. My first bonsai creation in that class was a pathetically deformed, miserable-looking Monterey Cypress, which I pampered and loved dearly. I miraculously survived such humble, bumbling beginnings and thereafter became hooked.

There were two Portuguese in the class, and I was included by them into an exclusive group of three, the Portuguese Bonsai Club. Membership was strictly limited: "You gotta either be one Portagee or you learned your bonsai from one Portagee." So I became the only buddhahead member. It was a start.

The bonsai treasure of Japan, Grand Master Kato Sensei, defined the three basic elements of *bonsai no kokoro* as (1) the relation of bonsai to nature, (2) the owner's relation to his bonsai and (3) the relation of bonsai lovers to each other. Bonsai is not only the replication of nature in the miniature but often manifests and emanates the healing touch of nature. Kato Sensei was heard to say, "*Bonsai wa kusuri* (Bonsai is medicine.)."

After returning from a hard day's work, eyes burning and shoulders aching, nothing brings the relief of relaxation of the nerves and body more than to dotingly water your plants. Why is it that when I am flu-stricken and ill at home, when I go outside to pull a few weeds, pinch off some sprigs and readjust some branches, the coughing stops and the sore throat and aching muscles disappear?

Surely, there must be a restorative, curative touch of nature in my plants, leading me to ponder whether there must not be a deeper, loftier meaning and perspective behind bonsai. I believe it starts with the owner's loving relationship with his trees, especially where he started it with a seedling or cutting and it has been trained and nurtured into a semblance of a bonsai. Then and thereafter it becomes like family. Even when a landslide crashed down on my bonsai, ripped off key branches, and disfigured their classic forms, I could not trash them any more than I could abandon a crippled child.

Bonsai can affect the broadening, bettering and enriching of the person, the character and the lives of all its spirit touches. As the Grand Master Kato declared: "We are united in the brotherhood of bonsai because bonsai is universal and a bond of brotherhood and friendship uniting all those who love bonsai, regardless of nationality, culture or race."

Bonsai can be a binding force even among those who differ, like the *yoseue* group planting comprised of many individual trees, each not of bonsai quality in itself but of different height, girth, shape and appearance then arranged, grouped and planted into one harmonious esthetic whole to form a beautiful forest composition and scene. The totality of an integrated, cohesive group, bonded and fused by common purpose and love of bonsai, becomes greater than any one of its parts.

When I started out, I searched for both plants and common bond with other bonsai enthusiasts. In 1965 I met Hideki Yonehara, a bonsai man who lived in Mānoa Valley. He was happy to meet a neophyte and share his love and knowledge of bonsai. He gave me his castoff plants to start my own bonsai collection. He also introduced me to additional practitioners from the original generation of bonsai men in Hawai'i. Unlike some of the old-timers who clutched their knowledge and techniques as esoteric secrets, "Papa" Kaneshiro proved to be unstinting and generous in giving his time, knowledge and techniques to us beginners. He shared the true spirit of bonsai no kokoro.

Soboku Nishihira, the rough and tough guy who introduced Papa Kaneshiro to bonsai, was another of the old-timers who willingly shared his bonsai and know-how with neophytes like me. I'll never forget how he described the strength and toughness of the *sotetsu* (sago palm) bonsai when he said: "Sotetsu just like Okinawa people. No drink water. No *kaukau*. Only suck the air and live!"

These were first-generation people who dated back to the 1920s in Hawai'i, around the time we Nisei were born. By making their acquaintance, taking notes, gaining their trust and finally writing articles about them, I can claim to be the surviving historical link between early bonsai in Hawai'i and bonsai as we know it today.

I read, learned, trained and experimented in all aspects of bonsai and became familiar with the common, scientific and Japanese names of bonsai tree material. During the '70s and '80s I reached the fever-pitched highs of the passion for bonsai that burned within me.

I particularly loved the *yamadori* of searching out and digging nature-shaped tree material from various locales, starting in the Kahuku hills with Papa Kaneshiro, then getting permission from sugar plantations at Makaweli, Olokele, Grove Farm, Lihue and Kilauea to dig ironwoods on Kaua'i, digging 'ōhi'a lehua from lava fields at Kapapalu Ranch and Hawai'i National Park on the Big Island, and even looking for *pemphis acidula* on Lana'i at the suggestion of my deer hunter friends. The best yamadori grounds turned out to be the Kalepa Ridge right behind the town of Hanamaulu, Kaua'i, the site of an old Civilian Conservation Corps soil preservation project during the Depression years where ironwood seedlings had been planted on the eroded red dirt hillside. They never grew over several feet due to poor soil and sparse rainfall and were perfectly dwarfed by nature. Our eyes virtually popped out of our heads when we first came upon this veritable nature's bonsai garden and saw the hillside covered with rows of stunted ironwood.

Among my yamadori partners, I particularly remember a great practitioner-friend, David Fukumoto, the day he and I stopped in Denver after a bonsai convention in Washington, D.C. We climbed the Rocky Mountain foothills to find magnificent weather-beaten, windswept, stunted junipers growing in rock crevices. They could not be dug out but only captured and preserved in color film. In those enthusiastic early years I imported evergreens, maple, elm, zelkova and other temperate zone trees from bonsai nurseries in Oregon and Washington.

Returning on my trips from Japan, I used to bring home five-needle pine (black pine was taboo), juniper, kaede maple and other quarantine-permissible bonsai and black pine seeds. I kept these cold-weather trees alive for extended periods in warm Hawai'i through my special dormancy experiments of "iceboxing" them in cold storage for several months, January to March, to mimic Japan's seasonal weather. I then brought these trees out and delighted in their explosive growth in the Hawaiian sunshine. Gradually though, these trees expired one by one when they discovered they had survived by artificial dormancy.

Over more than five decades of bonsai, I have grown, collected, purchased and trained several hundred bonsai. Fewer than fifty remain, none of exhibition quality. The ironwood and 'ōhi'a lehua collected on yamadori trips are long gone, and my favorite bonsai, the Japanese black pines, have expired one by one. My present collection is largely made up of the hardy Chinese Banyan and Taiwan Banyan varieties, which I train and shape into rock clinging *kengai* (cascade) forms and gift them to friends or charitable events as the source of my present-day bonsai kicks.

As for Kato Sensei's third key ingredient of bonsai, the relationships among growers, Papa Kaneshiro, Hideki Yonehara and other pioneers all belonged to the Honolulu Bonsai Kenkyu Club, to which I was introduced in 1968. While key individuals readily shared their knowledge, the bad news was that they operated the kenkyu club like a *kenjinkai*, a Japanese mutual aid association, with everything conducted Japanese-style in Japanese. Bonsai exhibits were plagued by inflamed competition, petty rivalry, argument and even fistfights when certain members had too much sake. Worst of all, the club had no educational purpose or program. So a small group of us, such as the botanist Horace Clay, David Fukumoto and myself, decided to peel off and form our own English-speaking bonsai organization, with a primary focus on bonsai education,

The Hawaii Bonsai Association (HBA) was chartered in 1970. Most fortuitously, Papa Kaneshiro came over to join us as our senior advisor. Dr. Clay, noted as a botany educator, served as our president for many years, and I served as secretary/treasurer. Beginning in 1970, HBA conducted a ten-week course called ABCs of Bonsai every year, sometimes twice a year, with an average enrollment of thirty to forty students. Our first ABCs class was conducted at the university, most memorable not for the bonsai instruction we imparted but for the distraction of an art class held in the floor below, which featured a live and fully unclothed Lady Godiva on a real horse, leaving our instructors hanging out the window instead of teaching students. For many years we have held two-hour a week classes from which the students proudly took home two self-trained bonsai. I originally served as a "director of education" of sorts, lecturing on the introductory phase, the basics of bonsai, and on shaping, trimming and wiring the trees for final potting. One of our crucial steps was in 1974, when we staged our first All-Oʻahu Bonsai Show at the Ala Moana Shopping Center stage area. Numerous affiliated clubs participated, and bonsai was exposed to some twenty thousand viewers over three days, starting a solid tradition of annual public exhibits.

Soon we went national and international. In the late 1970s we started attending bonsai conventions on the Mainland. There we first met and bonded with John Naka, America's foremost bonsai master, author of the text we used, *Bonsai Techniques*. In 1980, we hosted the annual Bonsai Club International, featuring John Naka as the premier master in America and Saburo Kato, the grand master of Japan.

The convention put our "tropical bonsai" onto the world bonsai map. BCI insisted that HBA sponsor decennial bonsai conventions, which we did in 1990 and 2000, attended by bonsai lovers from over the globe. The biggest event undertaken by HBA was to sponsor the BCI Bonsai Convention in year 2000 here in Hawai'i. It was attended by guests from over twenty different countries. It was most significant for me personally because the convention was dedicated to me, backed by proclamations from the state governor and legislatures and from various international bonsai organizations, such as Germany, Spain, South Korea, China and, of course, Japan.

I must tell you more about Sensei Kato. Notwithstanding the great stature and respect with which he was regarded in the bonsai world, all who knew him found him to be a warm, considerate, gracious, humble and beautiful human being. In stark contrast to certain people in the bonsai community who, with only superficial exposure, pridefully proclaim themselves to be experts, Sensei Kato once remarked that hardly a day passed in which he did not learn something new about bonsai.

In 1985, we formed the World Bonsai Friendship Federation, with Sensei Kato as chair. John Naka was vice chair and I was designated legal consultant, a role I occupied for many years. Horace Clay was also involved in the founding. Kato Sensei relied on me as his bridge to the English-speaking world by asking me to serve as translator for his lecture/demonstrations at conventions in Hawai'i; Omiya, Japan; Orlando, Florida; Barcelona, Spain; Seoul, South Korea; and Washington, D.C. In Spain I was regarded by the hosts as part of Kato Sensei's Japan entourage and was accordingly treated like bonsai royalty.

Our American network also formed the National Bonsai Foundation, which proposed building a tropical greenhouse conservatory at the National Arboretum in Washington, D.C. It was to be named in honor of Haruo Papa Kaneshiro, and I was appointed to chair the fund-raising in Hawai'i. We raised $130,000 for the Kaneshiro Conservatory, which was dedicated in October 1993. Alas, Papa did not live to see the first federal structure to be named for an Okinawan. Soon thereafter we launched a several million dollar project to renovate the Japan Bonsai Pavilion at the National Arboretum, which houses Japan's 1976 bicentennial gift of fifty Japan bonsai.

You can see this most pleasurable hobby was not marked by creating bonsai masterpieces but only by a trail of administrative and paperwork service. Nonetheless in 2001 that darned David Fukumoto filed a nomination with the Japanese Consulate in Hawai'i for me to receive an imperial award for my bonsai activities. The consulate received the nomination without much enthusiasm because they claimed their medals were not awarded "just for bonsai" until David pointed out that Japan already had given a medal to John Naka. David also got Kato Sensei to send in a letter of support. This got the consulate staff's attention big time and thereafter they begged David for more information on his nominee. So in ceremonies at the Japanese Consulate on July 14, 2001, attended by my whole family and special friends, the Japan government awarded me the Order of the Rising Sun, Silver Rays for promoting cultural exchange and friendship between the US and Japan.

I realized the warmth and depth of Kato Sensei's friendship when, unannounced, he and Mrs. Kato traveled from Japan to share in HBA's celebration of the Imperial Award, bearing an armful of gifts including a priceless scroll brushed in his own calligraphy with his gracious congratulatory message. I was dumbstruck that the most revered figure in bonsai would be willing to do all this for me! Words cannot describe the enrichment he has bestowed on my bonsai life. His sudden passing in December 2008 has left an irreparable void and emptiness in the world of bonsai and in mine that can never be filled nor replaced.

While bonsai was my most compelling lifelong form of recharge and recreation, it was far from the only one. Ever the frustrated athletic competitor, I became an avid and, as it's turned out, nearly lifelong golfer. At one point I obsessed over golf, read everything and thought deep thoughts about my swing. In my nineties, I shoot well under one hundred.

I also work out at the Nu'uanu YMCA several times a week. I work on several treadmill-like and weight machines and then swim thirty to forty laps in the pool, concentrating on deep breathing and remaining limber and sound.

At home, in addition to working with my fifty or so remaining bonsai, I do yardwork. It's important to do something every day. Some days, it may be as simple and rewarding as a long walk with Fuku.

Community Historian

After graduating from law school in 1950 and returning to Hawai'i to put down roots, for the next several decades I was too immersed in marriage, raising a family and establishing a professional livelihood to have the freedom of mind or time to pursue history. I did write about my church and contributed magazine articles on bonsai, but I circled my main subject, which was the nature and meaning of our wartime experience.

It was only as I achieved a measure of success in private practice that I was able to devote a substantial amount of my time to writing projects. With a broad agenda in mind, I began to systematically read and analyze contemporary history and to speak and write about what I found. I sensed that this coincided with a desire in the community to look back and assess what we had been through and what we had become. As a result, I incrementally found many venues and audiences without planning to do so.

My focus was the Nisei story in all its complexity. I was goaded by the question, "What did it mean, both to us who shared this experience and to the wider community and to history?"

I was preconditioned to ask such a question because I was raised with a strong awareness of history. My father was the historian of his family in Japan and also of our church in Hawai'i. He valued photography. From an early age, I was encouraged to write what I was learning. Reviewing my files, I was astonished to find a diary in Japanese that I wrote in 1939 as part of Japanese language school. My high school commencement and my talk at the point of departure of the VVV were exercises in writing and speaking. With my trusty Brownie camera, I somehow was the only VVV member who photographed our time at Schofield. I was sent out from Schofield to speak to the surrounding community about the VVV's work. While in army uniform, I wrote about winning the peace, about a new Hawai'i, and about the faraway places to which I had been deployed. At Indiana University, I wrote an essay on the history of Japanese in America. It seemed to really interest my classmates, who at the time knew virtually nothing about the subject.

My library of reading eventually filled five shelves. I collected every book, article and account I could find of the Nisei soldier, starting with John Tsukano's *Bridge of Love,* Chester Tanaka's *Go For Broke: A Pictorial History of the Japanese-American 100th Infantry Battalion and the 442nd Regimental Combat Team* and Joe Harrington's *Yankee Samurai: The Secret Role of Nisei in America's Pacific Victory* as well as many books about World War II. The resulting scholarship made me literate and knowledgeable on war history and contributed to my being regarded as having something to say.

Without intending to turn a corner, I went public with a talk I was asked to give commemorating Pearl Harbor Day 1977. I spoke at the request of the Association of the United States Army, which held a ceremony at the US Army Museum, which is located near Waikīkī Beach in an abandoned gun emplacement at Fort DeRussy, Hawai'i. The occasion was the Army's presentation of a battle streamer to the UH ROTC for being the first and only ROTC unit in the United States to be called to active duty in World War II.

My speech was titled "It All Started Here." I recounted how the UH ROTC responded to the call to service during the attack, our participation in the Battle of St. Louis Heights, our subsequent service in the Hawai'i Territorial Guard, our devastating dismissal from the HTG, the formation of the VVV and finally getting to the much better-known story of the 442nd Regimental Combat Team.

"It All Started Here" was well received. The editor of *The Honolulu Star-Bulletin,* Adam A. "Bud" Smyser, insisted that it be republished in the newspaper's 1978 Pearl Harbor anniversary issue. Retitled "Pearl Harbor Tragedy and Triumph," it laid out the basic theme and format for many speeches and articles that followed. Inevitably this anointed me with the enduring reputation of "war historian."

The *Star-Bulletin* had treated us Nisei with a certain amount of understanding in the war, and Bud Smyser kept that tradition going. After "It All Started Here," he published an article of mine in 1979 about the community figures who gave us crucial support in surviving the crisis. In 1982, I followed up with a closely related effort, a piece about the Emergency Service Committee, which was comprised of some of the most distinguished Japanese Americans of the war period, people whose contributions were previously not particularly well known.

One question arose repeatedly. Why did Japanese in Hawai'i and Japanese on the West Coast have such different experiences? Why were only a few people (fewer than one percent) interned in Hawai'i, while everyone was forced out of their homes and put in camps on the West Coast? To address this question, I co-authored yet another article for *The Honolulu Star-Bulletin* with the attorney Ellen Godbey Carson. Ellen is a civil rights lawyer who had been part of the legal team that overturned, in the US Supreme Court, the conviction of Fred Korematsu, who famously had refused to evacuate the West Coast. Our title was, "A Tale of Two Generals." We traced the infamous history of President Roosevelt's Executive Order 9066, which empowered area military commanders to evacuate anyone and everyone. General John L. DeWitt, in a panic and under pressure from the traditional anti-Japanese lobby, removed all people of Japanese ancestry from the Western Defense Command. In contrast, in Hawai'i, General Delos Emmons, to his great credit, nipped arrests in the bud and refused to engage in mass evacuations, despite pressure from Washington, D.C. to do so.

Smyser kindly acknowledged the essence of my motivation by writing, "Whenever Dec. 7, rolls around I think of Ted Tsukiyama. He thinks of 700 white crosses in Europe on V-E Day. They lurk in his memory and he works to keep the rest of us remembering, too."

Between writing and speaking, I was always more comfortable with writing. I have never been particularly articulate or voluble. Certainly I've never claimed to be an accomplished speaker or orator. But to reach an audience, the speaker's delivery must be effective. I detest and abhor reading a speech or listening to anyone else doing so. I prefer, even insist, that I look the listeners in the eye and talk to them, not at them, with knowledge, sincerity and conviction. I am inclined, even driven, to write out every speech, or at least to outline it, then go over it repeatedly until I know it by heart, which is the mark of the good speaker in conveying a meaningful message. The more I wrote, the more I was called upon to speak.

The movement to retrieve history was broadening in scope at the community level. Part of the reason was a centennial celebration in 1985, in which Governor George Ariyoshi, the first Japanese governor, provided leadership for a year-long reflection on the Japanese immigrant experience. The observance was called Kanyaku Imin, meaning "contract immigrants." By focusing on our founding generations, it tended to raise our cross-generational awareness.

I was the moderator/narrator of the last major event, a large community gathering held at the Blaisdell Auditorium called Kansha, which refers to gratitude. It was in the spirit of my first article for the *Star-Bulletin*. The event's goal was acknowledging non-Japanese individuals who had helped us through rough times. I faced my biggest audience, around eight thousand people, on December 1, 1985.

We honored twenty-four people in all, in the process illuminating large subjects of history. Two stand out. One was Charles Reed Hemenway. I detailed his life as the "father of the University of Hawai'i" and an influential business executive and community leader who befriended us long before the war and stood by us steadfastly and effectively during the war. Boldly using his immense prestige on our behalf, he formed a bridge to the martial law government and also to the elite haole community.

Hemenway's touch was personal: as witness the letters he repeatedly wrote to me while I was in Asia during the war.

Our references to him at the Kansha ceremony were necessarily brief, but I continued to honor Hemenway's memory. In his will, Hemenway had created a trust fund that financed scholarships for UH students decade after decade. I wrote and edited a biography booklet on him for the Hemenway scholarship program at UH, and

I served as a member of the scholarship committee along with Ralph Yempuku and others.

Among those still living in 1985, I went out of my way to talk about Hung Wai Ching. Hung Wai was there, full of life and verve. We heaped praise on him for his role as a member of the Morale Section, a founder of the Emergency Service Committee, the father figure of the VVV and a prime mover in organizing the 442. When he passed away in 2002 at the age of ninety-seven, I gave his eulogy. Of the many eulogies I gave in my career as a public speaker, it connected with the audience like no other. Everyone applauded.

With Hemenway as the facilitator and defender, Hung Wai Ching as a highly public advocate, and Morale Committee member Shigeo Yoshida as strategist, three people moved mountains to get us through the war. The three of them shaped our history on a monumental scale. Shigeo passed away in 1986 at age seventy-eight and, as with Hung Wai Ching, I was honored to give his eulogy.

On a trip to Washington, D.C. in the late 1980s I visited the National Archives (NARA) hoping to find some papers documenting how the VVV was formed to add authenticity and meaning to the history of the VVV. The military archivists could find nothing on the VVV but led me to Record Groups 107, 165 and others that preserved a treasure trove of military records, files and papers of the 100th Battalion and the 442nd Regimental Combat Team. I immediately resolved that all these records should be extracted and duplicated to form a 100th Bn./442nd RCT historical archive collection and made available in Hawaiʻi.

The noted archival researcher Aiko Yoshinaga Herzig was already engaged in the redress research project, which eventually unveiled the fact that the forced evacuation and removal from the West Coast was not a "military necessity," as it was always described. As a result of her prior commitment, Aiko was unavailable, but I got Richard "Sus" Yamamoto and his wife Fumi to accept the 100/442 research project at the National Archives. Starting in 1989, assisted by Maggie Ikeda and sometimes my sister Martha Giovanelli, the team paid weekly visits to NARA, poring through hundreds of files and extracting thousands of pages of records of the 100th and the 442, laboriously copying each page on Xerox machines, then packing these records into boxes that they mailed to me for filing with the 442nd archives.

The Yamamoto team continued their research for ten years until Dick Yamamoto was incapacitated with severe arthritis, during which time they produced over twenty-five lineal feet of military papers, the largest archival collection of 100th/442nd records outside of the National Archives in Washington, D.C. The Yamamoto team did this without receiving a cent of compensation for their time and services while I got the local 100th and 442 clubs to fund the costs of Xeroxing and mailing the records. This Yamamoto Archival Collection now reposes in the 100th and 442nd archives, with a duplicate set donated to the Nisei Veterans Archive Center of the UH Hamilton Library. From around 2005, the NARA research project was taken over by a volunteer research team from the Japanese American Veterans Association (a Maryland-based organization), including Fumi Yamamoto. It completely recovered all 100/442 records and expanded its search to Military Intelligence Service records. I consider my part in the initiation of this project to be one of the most significant and rewarding efforts toward preserving the historical legacy of the war.

All the while I continued writing and speaking with the goal of putting my researches to wide public use. The early 1990s were the fiftieth anniversary years of the various Japanese American units. For their anniversary observances, I became heavily involved in developing publications aimed at digging deeper into their origins and marking their sacrifices and achievements.

I was continuously motivated by the comparative reticence of most of my comrades and buddies. Many of them understandably did not want to dwell on the war. Some thought silence was a virtue. Worse, veterans clammed up even with their children, often more so with their children than others. For that reason I eventually gave a talk aimed at encouraging the next generation to pry information out of my generation. It was titled "Talk To Me, Dad!" and was part of an AJA Veterans Convention Oral History Workshop.

I practiced what I preached, gathering many oral histories on my own, including a massive oral history of Hung Wai Ching well before his passing.

Through formation of something we called the Nikkei History Editorial Board, we encouraged many others to write. The result was a book series, *Japanese Eyes American Heart*. Volume I was an anthology of the experiences of sixty Nisei soldiers. My contribution was a four-page article titled "An American—Not a Japanese Living in America." Volume II branched out more into the community. As I write, a broadly based Volume III is in the works.

There were many other moments on this path, too numerous to describe in any detail. I talked to the Bamboo Ridge Writer's Institute (where Fuku was the "mother hen" of a vital literary group). I spoke at the dedication ceremony of the Military Intelligence Service Monument at Punchbowl National Cemetery. I also spoke to a good many university classes—for example, the UH ROTC class and a UH Ethnic Studies class. More than once, I spoke to both the 442nd RCT annual dinner and various workshops of the Sons and Daughters of the 442.

In 1984, the Japanese American Citizens League held its annual convention in Hawai'i. I titled my talk "Whither JACL-Hawai'i?" to focus what I perceived as an identity crisis facing the Japanese in Hawai'i. Paraphrasing, I created a pidgin English poem, "The Soliloquy of Hamlet Yamato," that climaxed with the deathless words: "...Ma name Ameriken, ma face Japanee. So wat! As up to me, To be free an' make it in Hawai'i. So, fak you, you faka, I goin' be shaka!" which brought down the house.

In 1996, I delivered a talk in Japanese to the Fuchu City (Japan) Students Group. With my lousy grasp of the language, I really sweated that one out, but I was complimented for my efforts.

Various citations came my way, which always had to do with my upholding and developing the voice for the many who remained silent. I was touched to be named a distinguished alumnus of the University of Hawai'i and a living treasure in the opinion of Honpa Hongwanji Buddhist mission.

Much about our society changed across the decades. I remember once saying of a local election, "There are no more dragons left to slay." Dating to 1954, the Democratic Party long since had taken over the politics of Hawai'i, led by Japanese Americans at every level, including US Senators Daniel K. Inouye and Spark M. Matsunaga, as well as Patsy Takemoto Mink in the US House of Representatives. Jack Burns, a stalwart supporter in wartime, was elected to three four-year terms as governor beginning in 1962. His successor, George Ariyoshi, was not only the first Japanese American governor but the first nonwhite to be elected governor of an American state. Similarly, the battle for labor representation is long-since won.

The events of the VVV, the HTG and the 442 that were so vividly real for me and my generation are in danger of becoming ancient history or even a past that is unknown to today's young people. In the belief that all will not be forgotten, I hold up this story as a chapter in Hawai'i's history, and as a page in America's, in which Hawai'i and the nation took a step forward.

As I write, most of my buddies and wartime comrades are now deceased.

On September 3, 2014, my dear Fuku passed away, at the age of eighty-nine. The memory of our rich life together is always with me.

Appendix

Writings and References

"The Inside Story: From Tragedy to Triumph," December 7, 1979—*Honolulu Star-Bulletin* acknowledges Robert L. Shivers, Kendall J. Fielder, Charles Hemenway and Hung Wai Ching as key persons who stood up for the loyalty and trustworthiness of Hawai'i's Japanese and helped to avert the tragedy of mass evacuation from Hawai'i.

"Behind The War Clouds: A Story of Unsung Valor and Devotion," April 9, 1982—*Honolulu Star-Bulletin* recognizes the Hawai'i Nisei leaders who formed and served in the Emergency Service Committee.

"Nisei Military Experience During World War II," May 21, 1988—East-West Center Conference on Cultural Encounters in the Pacific War, covering the prewar suspicion and distrust of Hawai'i's Japanese, the HTG, VVV, 100/442nd RCT and MIS.

"A Tale of Two Generals" (co-authored with Ellen Godbey Carson) December 2, 1991—*Honolulu Star-Bulletin* reveals the contrasting application of Executive Order 9066 regarding evacuation/internment by General DeWitt (Western Defense Command) and General Emmons (Hawaiian Command).

We Remember Pearl Harbor by Lawrence Rodriggs, September 1, 1991—recounts Ted Tsukiyama's wartime experience (pages 243–256).

"The Nisei Legacy," August 15, 1992, UH symposium for 442 Sons and Daughters, a speech also given October 6, 1992—Elderhostel Educational Program.

"A Salute To The One Puka Puka," history and tribute to the 100th Infantry Battalion for the Go For Broke album of the 442nd fiftieth anniversary, March 23, 1993.

"Origins of the 442," Go For Broke album of the 442nd fiftieth anniversary, March 23, 1993.

"The Nisei Intelligence War Against Japan," 1993, published by MIS Historical Committee of MIS Veteran's Club of Hawai'i (editor Ted Tsukiyama)—a thirty-three-page history of the formation, training and combat service of Nisei graduates of the Military Intelligence Service Language School, Camp Savage, Minnesota, to the various combat zones against the Japanese enemy.

"Secret Valor," July 8, 1993, album of Hawai'i Nisei linguists fighting the intelligence war against the Japanese military on Asia-Pacific battlefields as well as in the occupation of postwar Japan, MIS Veteran's Club of Hawai'i fiftieth anniversary reunion album (editor Ted Tsukiyama).

"The 100th/442nd Legacy," February 25, 1995, Sons and Daughters of the 442nd—an informal dialogue recalling the HTG and VVV precursors of 442nd RCT/100th Bn.

"The Nisei MIS Story," March 11, 1995, Sons and Daughters of the 100th/442nd/MIS—dialogue of why and how the MIS was formed and its service in the war against Japan.

"The American Nikkei Soldier of World War II," August 24, 1995, Nikkei Hei Gojunen Kinen Kai—a speech delivered to a Japanese group in Japanese.

"Fiftieth Anniversary Celebration of War's End," August 1995.

"Nisei War Experiences," 1996—a personal view.

"Our Bridges Of Love," December 6, 1996, *The Hawai'i Herald*—a story of the personal bridges of love, goodwill and friendship created by the 442nd with people of Italy, France and Germany.

"Hawai'i's Nikkei Soldiers: Why Did They Fight."

"A Spy In Their Midst: The Saga of Richard M. Sakakida," 1998—written for the book *Japanese Eyes American Heart*, published as "Secret Mission" pages 163–169, subsequently edited for "Fire For Effect: A unit history of the 522nd Field Artillery Battalion."

Appendix 157

"The 522nd Field Artillery Battalion," including the lead article pages 5–16, 31–76 and "The 522nd Encounter with the Holocaust" (pages 59–70), about Nisei liberation of the Jewish prisoners of the Dachau Death March and Dachau subcamps.

Japanese Eyes American Heart, 1998—an anthology of the experiences of sixty Nisei soldiers, Hawai'i Nikkei History Editorial Board (member Ted Tsukiyama), including "An American—Not a Japanese Living in America" (pages 335–339).

"The Battle of Okinawa Revisited," 1999—a hundred-page essay of the epic last battle of the Pacific War from a US military perspective, a Japanese perspective, an Okinawa victim's perspective and the combat service of the Nisei MIS and the postwar contribution to Okinawa (condensed version at website: www.nisei.hawaii.edu).

"The Varsity Victory Volunteers: Pioneer AJA Unit of World War II," February 23, 2002—an updated story on the VVV sixtieth anniversary reunion.

"100th/442nd Battlefields Revisited," August 6, 2004, *The Hawai'i Herald*—a journal account of a K Company Tour of 2004 revisiting the battlefields of the Gothic Line mountains in Italy and France including the site of the Lost Battalion Rescue and concluding with a visitation of the US Military Cemetery at Epinal.

"The Nisei Intelligence War Against Japan," October 12, 2004, updated.

"Who You Goin' Shoot?" October 24, 2004, Bamboo Ridge Writer's Institute Workshop.

"UH ROTC Homecoming/Reunion," December 7, 2005—a speech tracing the formation of the 442nd to the UH ROTC, HTG and VVV.

"OSS Detachment 101," December 1, 2006, *The Hawai'i Herald*—on the secret Nisei guerrilla unit that tormented the Japanese Army in Burma, including VVV friends Ralph Yempuku, Junichi Buto, Chiyoki Ikeda, Calvin Tottori.

"The Loyalty Oath," 2006, 442nd Go For Broke bulletin—a story of the contrasting treatment of the infamous loyalty oath (DSS Form 304A) by Nisei on the Mainland versus those in Hawai'i.

"522nd Liberates Kaufering IV Hurlach," 2007, 442nd Go For Broke bulletin—an updated sequel to the Ichiro Imamura account of the liberation of a Dachau subcamp.

"Hawai'i's Nisei Soldiers of World War II," February 27, 2011, MIS Veterans Club Shinen Kai luncheon acknowledging little known Nisei soldiers and units, published in Hawai'i Pacific Press.

"Shigeo Yoshida: Unsung Hero of the Home Front," March 2011, in *Japanese Eyes American Heart, Volume II*, also stories on Goro Arakawa, Chito Isonaga, Sue Isonaga, Nadao Yoshinaga and Wilfred Oka (book published December 11, 2012).

"VVV," December 11, 2012, *Japanese Eyes American Heart, Volume II*.

"Sempai Gumi," 2012, Puka Puka (100th) Parade—on the fifty-nine Nisei of the 100th Bn. transferred from the 442 to MIS Language School.

December 7, 2012—The VVV (Varsity Victory Volunteers), a capsulized summary of the VVV written for the 442nd Foundation 2012 Annual Report.

"Chu Naran To…" December 13, 2015—an article based on the television show *Taira No Kiyomori* tying together ancient Japanese feudal history with Nisei valor during World War II, submitted to the MIS bulletin.

"Answering The Call," November 11, 2013—speech delivered on Veteran's Day aboard the USS *Missouri*.

Feature Articles

"Charles Reed Hemenway," January 15, 1984—a booklet tribute to the legendary friend.

"Henry," January 15, 1991—a short story about my hospital roommate, a derelict who was lovingly cared for by the nursing staff.

"Chiune Sugihara: A 'Schindler' of Japan," October 7, 1994, *The Hawai'i Herald*—the story of a Japanese diplomat who issued visas facilitating the escape of many Jews from Nazi Europe.

"What Yale Law Has Meant To Me," October 6, 1995, Yale Law School Class of 1950 reunion directory.

"Jesse S. Shima: Issei Pioneer—Benevolent American," April 4, 2003, *The Hawaiʻi Herald*.

"Eyewitness To History: From Pearl To Hiroshima, Mitsuko Masaki Sumida Was Touched by The War," December 2, 2005, *The Hawaiʻi Herald*—an article about the historic Fukunaga case including the heroic but futile appeal by Attorney Robert Murakami.

"Rusty and Me," January 31, 2010, *The Hawaiʻi Herald*—a tribute to my faithful dog, Rusty.

"Okage Sama De," May 10, 2012—acknowledgment of Lifetime Achievement Award, UH Alumni Association banquet.

"I Respectfully Dissent," December 1, 2012, 442nd bulletin—a book review of the biography of Justice Edward Nakamura (HTG, VVV and 442nd).

"The Japanese in Hawaiʻi Labor History," December 7, 2012—submitted for publication to *The Hawaiʻi Herald*.

"442nd and Culture Shock," March 7, 2013—based on the thesis that serving in the 442nd was a liberating experience for the Nisei soldier.

"OSS Nisei Liberate Japanese POW Camps," April 26, 2013—the story of OSS Nisei who flew mercy missions to liberate American prisoners in POW camps.

Acknowledgments

The author would like to thank all of those who helped make this book possible, especially Tom Coffman for his invaluable contributions to the text and Atsuko Igarashi, who assisted with the spelling of Japanese names.